Today's Revenue and Profit Acceleration Strategies

Immediate Profit-Enhancing Strategies

for Today's Business

by George Farrall

COPYRIGHT AND DISCLAIMER

DEDICATION

I would like to dedicate this book to all the business owners and leaders that are ready to achieve their business goals and dreams.

To my family, friends, mentors, advisers, teachers, and everyone else that allowed me to gain the knowledge and insight to assist businesses thrive and survive.

To Your Success,

George Farrall

CONTENTS

Introduction

The purpose of this book is to walk you through a process I have created where I can show you the strategic profit acceleration techniques you can use to increase your company's revenue and profits.

I will go through strategies that are proven profit-generators for any business. Most business owners know nothing about these strategies, and therefore, are failing to capitalize on their profit-generating power.

For the purposes of this book, I'll cover each of the strategies in individual chapters for one main reason. I want you to be able to review these strategies and minimize the amount of time it will take you to implement them in their entirety.

But consider this...the pandemic crisis and the upcoming recession has business owners today in the fight of their lives. The global economy is in shambles, they have no additional revenue sources they can tap into for financial support during lean times – and perhaps worst of all, marketing and advertising just don't work as well as they used to. In fact, for many business owners, marketing isn't producing any results for them at all... and their financial situation is growing more desperate by the day.

As a business owner or entrepreneur, if you're struggling right now to generate more leads and clients for your business, and you need to find immediate ways to dramatically increase your business' bottom-line revenue, then spend the next few minutes with me and I'll show you how I can help you make all of these problems disappear forever.

As you follow the book and read the principles to follow, remember it does not matter what industry nor type of business you operate. What matters is you use these principles, lessons, and strategies to grow your revenue and profits.

The best time to start is NOW, not tomorrow, not next week or next month.

To Your Success,

George Farrall

The Surprising Impact of a Little Strategic Research

In this chapter, we'll look at the strategic nature of studying your competition and studying businesses *outside* of your competitive landscape. Let's first begin with the study of your competitors.

The Study of Competitors

This information will help you in the following ways:

A) It is my experience that even when there is a difference between one business and another, most businesses do not know how to communicate it. If there isn't any differentiation between your business and other similar businesses, you must find something that you can differentiate your business so that you stand out in the minds of potential customers. Knowing your competition will help you build a strategy to grow your market share.

B) If another competing business has double the number of customers, you want to ask the questions, "What are they doing that I am not? How can I incorporate what they're doing in my business?" That alone will give you leverage as you improve your marketing.

If you are ahead of others on that spectrum, you will be able to teach others outside of your competitive area what you do because you probably have a method, technique, or process that hundreds or thousands of other people in your direct industry would pay an ongoing usage fee, percentage, or training fee to learn, because it gives them greater leverage in their businesses.

You must clearly identify what you do well and what you do poorly. If you do it better than anyone else, you can teach others. If you do it worse than other people, you have to identify what they do and incorporate it. This simple realization could easily add 20% or 30% to your revenues.

Simply stated, the missing element for many businesses who attempt any form of marketing is research! It's not fun! It's tedious. But it's all important.

I can't do your research for you, but I can give you great questions to ask so that you can do your own research. Or, if you are too busy, you can hire someone else to do this for you and then present to you a detailed report of their findings. Business school students would be ideal to ask because you can get them at a low cost, but you also know that they have learned how to research for the projects that their professors give them.

Here are the questions you must find the answers for if you want to dominate:

1. Can you clearly identify who else is providing the same or similar products or services?
2. Do you know what their market share is?
3. Do you know if their market share has been declining or growing in the past five years?
4. Can you give specific numbers?
5. Do you know if the number of similar businesses is increasing or declining?
6. Given the previous answer, what do you project the number of similar businesses to be in the next year? (An estimate is okay.)
7. After five years?
8. Can you list all your competitors by name?
9. Do you know what their Market Dominating Positions or USPs are?
10. Is there a clear differentiation about your product or service?
11. How does your business differ from the competition in terms of pricing?
12. Are you aware of what other similar businesses are offering that you don't?
13. Do you know how they communicate in ways that you don't?
14. Do you know what means of marketing they use that you don't?
15. Do you know what means of marketing they use that you do, but that they use more efficiently?
16. Are you currently taking steps to offset the advantages that your competitors have?
17. Have you taken steps in the past?
18. What were the results of those steps?
19. Do you know what your competitors' biggest weaknesses or failings are?
20. Do you specifically compensate for that failing so that you gain market share?

If you have a team working for you that develops your marketing, ask them these same questions. Don't settle for vague or simple verbal answers. Demand the results on paper in a report. This will separate those who are just playing at marketing from those who are serious about building your business.

If you are a one-man show, or a one-woman show, you still must do this work. Again, how serious are you about growth?

The Study of Non-Competitors

There is an ancient text that says, "Make the most of every opportunity." This is a great reminder for those of us in business that we need to optimize. Your goal should not only be to make the most of every opportunity you have, but also of

- your capital,
- your time,
- your facilities,
- your staff,
- your equipment,
- and your goodwill.

You can't "make the most" until you understand the wide range of possibilities that are available.

Most people spend their whole lives in one field of work and all they know is the field they are in. It's like traveling the world. You leave your small town and go to the big city, and you see and experience all types of new things. You find that people in the big city do things a little differently and perhaps are more effective in certain areas than you because they utilize different methods, systems, or bases of knowledge.

However, then you find that people in other areas of the country might do things 20% or 30% or 50% differently. Then you travel to other countries on the same side of the world and discover greater variations. Then you travel to any other 20 points in the world and find another 20 different, but effective, systems.

If you only learn from your own industry in your own (relatively) small part of the country, you are limiting yourself to the smallest fraction of the yield that you might possibly make. Business owners in New York can learn sales and marketing strategies from other business owners in the same state, but can also learn from dentists in New Zealand, insurance salespeople in Australia, clothing store owners in England, and investment bankers in Hong Kong. This ultimately leads us to the concept of Mastermind Groups, first detailed in print by Napoleon Hill—getting together with astute businesspeople from diverse environments to expand your own ability to conduct business.

Just because everyone in our county operates their business the same way does not mean that it is the most efficient, enjoyable, or profitable way. You must step outside and look at more powerful alternatives that others may have discovered outside your field, then pull them back in and adapt them to your current situation.

Most people don't have the right mindset and think that a more efficient, enjoyable, or profitable way is impossible. Unless they change their mindset to believe in the possible and achievable, their lives will forever be the same and they'll always be playing "catch-up". You must change the way you do something, or your outcome will always be the same. One of my favorite quotes (presumably by Ben Franklin—though some attribute it to Einstein) is:

> *"The definition of insanity is doing the same thing over and over again but expecting different results."*

You should realize that it's probable that there are people out there in your field who have already discovered far more powerful, efficient, profitable, and enjoyable ways of doing things than you are aware of. There is no reason that you must reinvent the wheel yourself. It's much easier and safer to borrow proven, successful strategies and processes from outside your field and apply them to your business practice. They have the highest possibility of improving your results and the lowest possibility of wasting your money.

Most people spend their whole life in one field, and this creates a problem. They become an expert at what their industry teaches, but this becomes the major bulk of their sphere of knowledge. Their industry does not necessarily operate at maximum productivity or efficiency. Most of what these people do is learned from someone else in the same industry and no one gets better.

Tunnel vision may be hurting your business, but funnel vision will bring you great success. If all you know is what your industry knows, this is tunnel vision. You must realize that there might be 20, 200 or 2,000 other ways to market your business, to gain new customers, and to make a profit, and you need to borrow the success secrets wherever you can find them. By doing so, you give yourself much greater leverage.

You want an exponential, quantum leap advantage over other businesses and studying the marketing processes of businesses outside your industry is a powerful way to get it.

Open your eyes. I believe it was Mark Joyner (Internet Marketing guru) who said, "When you walk into a store and you don't come out with a new marketing idea, then you're asleep."

When you fire up Google or YouTube and you haven't learned something new about marketing, then you are not living consciously.

Live with your eyes open. Take notes. Implement. Test. Try again.

The Power of Strategy and Its Ability to Dominate Your Market

Let me start with a question that I hope will stimulate your thinking.

What's the simplest, fastest way to quickly produce tangible results that grow your business beyond your imagination?

Stated another way, if you could only do one thing, what is that one thing you would do that would bring you the result you need?

Remember this: The right strategy will *always* overcome time, effort, and capital.

Sometimes, business owners with too much money do stupid things. They buy their way out of a problem with an all-too-easy approach, rather than take the time to come up with a strategy that could shift their entire business. The result is that they compete with the other players in the market on the same playing field, rather than elevate themselves into an altogether new atmosphere.

I have a book on my desk called "The Power of Broke" by Daymond John, one of the stars of Shark Tank. In the book, he shows the reader how those who are broke must dig deep to find creative solutions to solve problems, not just dive into their bank account.

I think of Robert Allen who wanted to grow in national prominence. His strategy was to show people how to buy property with no money down. His tactic which he used successfully was to write a press release that said, "Send me to any city, take away my wallet, and in 72 hours I'll buy an excellent piece of property using none of my own money."

He got a terrific amount of media attention, and it catapulted his career into the stratosphere. No other real estate agent could touch that.

That's the power of a great strategy!

It'd be nice to find an angle that gets national media attention but that's not always possible. A breakthrough strategy doesn't have to be on a nation-wide scale; it just must be something that your competitors aren't doing.

When you take on new customers, you want to be a hero to those customers. You want to give them a massive advantage over what your competitors might give them.

You might think that hard work is what is going to save your business, but that's not entirely true. Again, a good strategy will *always* overcome effort, time, and capital. If you have the wrong strategy, you can work 18 hours a day and sink all your money into your business, and you will still lose your shirt.

Let me give you an example. Perhaps most businesses in a niche have a weak strategy and just "sell, sell, sell". But one business has a nurturing and educational strategy where they position themselves as the market educators. Then every marketing piece they release is informative and useful to their target market and it positions them as *the* experts in the market. People want to do business with the experts, not those who are just the same as everyone else. Expert positioning leads to trust and trust leads to increased sales.

Do you see how that business will dominate the industry over time? Consider also that if you find a great strategy, you'll do so much better if you stick to it and not get sidetracked.

The Bottom Line

The unfortunate truth is that the subject of strategy is also infinite and that coming up with prize-winning ideas takes wisdom and experience. You must study a lot about how different companies have faced challenges and then overcome them to find breakthroughs.

Innovation can include new ideas, technologies, methods, products, and services that help your business make more revenue and/or profit. How are you encouraging your staff or employees to think more innovatively so that your business remains competitive?

Along the same line, you can also ask yourself, "Is it rewarding them with authority, rank, recognition, prizes, or money?"

As a business owner, it's not up to you to come up with all the answers. You have an entire team that could be motivated to bring in fresh ideas. If the Lifetime Value of one of your clients is $1,200, what would you be willing to reward your employees if they came up with ideas to bring in more customers, or serve them at a higher level which increases the lifetime value?

You might think, "They should just be doing it. It's a part of their job."

But I would argue this: "They aren't doing it. So how could you motivate them to do it?"

If I were to put myself in the shoes of one of your salesclerks and you came to the staff and said, "I have ten $100 bills for the person who brings me the best idea to grow our business this week that we could actually implement," I'd go home to my family and friends and say, "Please help! I need to come up with a great idea because there's a $1,000 reward for it."

Here's the result. You now have several more people thinking hard about how to grow your business and you only have to reward them if they come up with a great idea that you can actually use.

Now we come to the question which I'll give credit to the late Chet Holmes. I've asked this question for years to my clients and there is *always* breakthrough to be found here.

What are your ultimate strategic objectives?

When you go into a sales meeting, what do you want to accomplish? Most people say, "I want to make the sale."

That's well and good but what *else* would you like to accomplish?

Some people have told me that they'd like to get referrals or build a relationship. More often than not, people don't know what else to do.

I believe that there are at least 16 things you could accomplish on that sales call. Let me give you some examples:

1. To be *the* source of innovative ideas.
2. To be known as a business of the highest integrity.
3. To be the most sought after for help and information.
4. To have a growing number of residual clients.
5. To be the business that sets the criteria by which people buy.
6. To build brand loyalty (to ourselves) on purpose.
7. To treat people as *clients* that we care for, not *customers that we sell to.*
8. To be, and be known as, *the* experts in our industry.
9. To build the highest credibility.
10. To have clients like us.
11. To have clients trust us.
12. To have clients respect us.
13. To motivate clients to buy more of what is good for them.
14. To arm clients with powerful information that they can share with others.
15. To pre-empt and dis-empower the competition.
16. To build our referrals as a natural engine of growth.

Imagine if you took just 3 or 4 of these strategic objectives and you ensured that they were incorporated into all your marketing activities, your website, your brochures, your emails, your scripts, your sales calls! *Influence is the Result!*

You'll also likely grow your business by at least 10%, simply by ensuring that your strategic objectives are incorporated in all your marketing tactics.

However, if you are *already* doing this, ask yourself this question:

Does your strategy include creating and making compelling offers at various stages of The Buyer's Journey?

The **Buyer's Journey** is a "map" that helps you understand the "journey" that a buyer goes through before they make a purchase. There are 3 main stages: Awareness, Consideration, and Decision. Each stage of the journey requires a different marketing and sales approach.

In the **Awareness Stage**, a prospect may be unaware of their need and unaware of your company and your ability to meet their need. In this phase, you'll want to lean heavily on educational content, e-books, research reports, and analyst reports. Which ones do you have?

Awareness Stage

Type of Material	Already Exists	Need to Create
Educational Content	Yes/No	Yes/No
E-book		
Research Report		
Analyst Report		
Other		

In the **Consideration Stage**, the prospect is now aware of their need and your presence, and they begin their research into all their options for a solution. You'll want to use marketing material such as expert guides, comparison white papers, webinars, and videos. Which ones do you have?

Consideration Stage

Type of Material	Already Exists	Need to Create
Expert Guides	Yes/No	Yes/No
Comparison White Papers		
Webinars		
Videos		
Other		

In the **Decision Stage**, the prospect is trying to decide between you and your competitor. Use case studies, testimonials, trial offers, comparisons against competitors, and live demos.

Decision Stage

Type of Material	Already Exists	Need to Create
Case Studies	Yes/No	Yes/No
Testimonials		
Trial Offers		
Comparisons Against Competitors		
Live Demonstrations		
Other		

It's a rare company that has compelling offers through each stage of the Buyer's Journey. With that in mind, if you could build marketing and sales material for each aspect of the Buyer's Journey, by what percent do you think that would impact your growth?

Concluding Thought

Author Naveen Jain wrote, "Success doesn't necessarily come from breakthrough innovation but from flawless execution. A great strategy alone won't win a game or a battle; the win comes from basic blocking and tackling." For your business, success won't come from your bright ideas; it will come from your ability to help your staff implement them relentlessly over an extended period.

How to Grow Your Business by Building Trust Through an Expert Positioning Strategy

In this chapter, I'm going to help you position yourself as the expert and, more importantly, *why*. I'll also share how to implement an education-based marketing strategy, and then how you can even get your prospects to pay you to solicit them.

My goal in this chapter is to make it as concise as possible, so you can apply it to your business in an ordered manner and begin to make increased profits, both in the short-term and in the long-term.

Let's look at several reasons why we want to look at expert positioning and education. First, have you heard of **Milgram's Law**? It's a business principle, or law, which states that *"People will blindly believe the words of an expert."*

Now I am assuming you are an honest and ethical businessperson, and you will only use this for good. But think about this: there was a time when people believed every word that was printed in the newspaper because the newspaper was considered an expert source. Still, today, if someone who is a well-known teacher speaks on a certain topic, most people will blindly believe the teaching as truth, without taking the time to do the study themselves.

And most times that's okay. We translate that to our business environment. If you purposefully position yourself as *the* expert, and people come to recognize your expertise, then they will believe what you tell them, regardless of whether it's true or not.

> **Your expert positioning is built on education.**
>
> **It is *not* built on advertising.**
>
> **Advertising does *not* build trust.**
>
> **Education builds trust.**

And this is of critical importance, and I'll show you the reason shortly.

There's a second law. It's called **Zipf's Law** and it states that *"In an over-crowded marketplace, your potential client will naturally choose the option of the leader <u>perceived</u> to be on top."*

The key idea here is "perception". People are desperate for someone to lead them and if you lead people with education and with authority, they will gladly follow you. You then give yourself distinction because very few others are doing this and if you are competing in an over-crowded marketplace, then you will come out on top as the natural leader.

A little caveat of warning here: if you want to take this position, you had better have some good material to solidify your position. There will always be a group of people who want to challenge, or test, your leadership. If you do your homework, then you will have a lot less trouble. People are desperate for someone to follow, but the kind of followers you want are not idiots. They will ask you a few questions so that they can satisfy their minds about your level of expertise. Expect this. Know your material. Respond with intelligence and you'll come out shining.

As a business coach/consultant, an exercise that I have developed is to understand the meaning or definition of 35 or 40 terms, know the impact that each one can have on a business, then understand how to apply them to specific situations. So, if someone comes up to me and says, "*Can you explain the difference between upsell, cross-sell and downsell?*" I can say, "*It means this, this and this, and here's why it's important to apply these in a business.*"

A wise man once said, "*In the land of the blind, the one-eyed man is king.*" You may not feel that your level of expertise is anything to boast about, but if you know more about one area of your business than most others in your industry, then you are an expert to many. Positioning yourself as an industry expert is a strategic move that has a very powerful effect on the marketplace. Most people love to be led and advised by someone who is an authority.

Your position as *the* expert brings you respect. In fact, you may not even have a greater knowledge about some aspects of your business, but if you are the first business to educate your marketplace about the benefits of your product or service, you will be *perceived* as the expert and you will gain market share.

The perception of an industry expert brings trust;

trust helps people act.

Let's shift this a little bit to talk about *education*. Whether you position yourself as the industry expert or not, it is vitally important that you take the time to educate every customer or prospective customer. Most business owners assume too much. They think (often mistakenly) that their prospective customers already know everything that there is to know about their product or service.

The more those customers understand *every* dimension of your product or service, the more comfortable they will feel when they cross that psychological or emotional bridge to make the purchase.

Education increases the perception of value.

With increased value comes the ability to either raise your prices or sell a greater quantity of your product or service at the same price.

Education always deals in specifics, not generalities. You can't simply say, "This is the best product in the country" (unless it truly is, and you can show people exactly why your statement is true). Otherwise, customers will know that you are exaggerating, and they will not likely trust further statements you make.

Specific information breeds trust and validity. Consequently, greater trust leads to greater profits.

Here's a key point to note: The more expensive the item, or the more complex your service, the more you need to educate. If you are selling simple widgets, then you don't need to educate much at all. If you are selling a computer software package, then you will need to educate much more.

Many people think that sales letters or advertisements should be very short and succinct. I want to challenge that idea. Think about a salesman going into the home of Mrs. Jones and he's trying to sell her a product or service. Could the salesman do a better job of selling in 3 seconds, in 30 seconds, in 3 minutes, or in 30 minutes?

It's clear that the answer is 30 minutes. 3 seconds is enough for a prospect to read your slogan and capture interest, but it doesn't close a sale.

30 seconds is not much better. It builds interest and perhaps makes the prospect hungry to learn more.

3 minutes is better still, but you will still have a prospect with questions and doubts that need to be satisfied.

30 minutes will clearly give you the best chance of making a sale. You have time to build a presentation, build rapport, qualify the buyer, build value, create desire, handle objections, close the sale and show the buyer that you'll be following up. And *voila*! Those are the 7 steps to the sale!

Here's the key point I'm building up to: You won't often make a sale on the first contact with a prospect. Yes, there are 3% - 10% of prospects who are buying now, and you might get lucky and find one of those. However, you can build an education-based marketing strategy so that you:

- Build rapport over time,
- Build value over time,
- Create increased desire over time,
- Gain their trust over time,
- Answer objections over time.

And you do all of this through education, not through selling.

I'm going to give you a specific process so that you can implement this strategy in three different ways. You can choose what is right for your business and you'll have a template to follow so you can get to work today and have this implemented in your business right away. Before we can get to those three ways, we have some steps to consider.

First Step: Ask yourself these questions, and make a list of every distinction that you can think of:

1. What processes, experience, wisdom, technology, or information make possible this product or service that I offer? This doesn't have to be information that is specific *only* to your business. It can be information that everyone in the industry has access to. You might think of it as "common knowledge" but record it anyway because there may be many outside your industry (i.e., Mr. and Mrs. Prospect) that don't really understand this "common knowledge".
2. How are they unique, interesting, or impacting? Write down the areas that would especially be beneficial to your prospect. List the features on one side of your page and the

corresponding benefits on the other side of the page.

3. Which ones are my customers not likely to be fully aware of?
4. How can I better communicate these in a way that will be appreciated or valued?

Second Step: Remember who your typical, ideal client is. This will make a big difference in how you approach people and what you say, so if you haven't done your research, I would encourage you again to get it done. You can still implement this strategy of education and expert positioning, but you'll be doing it with one hand and one foot tied behind your back.

You can still win the game if your competitors are mediocre, but if you come up against a competitor who is taking this seriously... well, as they say, "*You have as much chance of winning as a one-legged man in a butt-kicking contest.*"

This can go in a couple different directions and we're going to cover each one for you so you can choose. You can deliver this education as:

- Seminars
- Books, podcasts, video lessons, whitepapers, magazine articles (or article series), radio or TV shows, newsletters, or series of letters.

Let's look at each of these.

Seminars

One of the fastest ways to catapult your "expert positioning" to the top is to put on seminars or events. I sometimes use the word "event" because it gives a different perception than that of a seminar.

Remember what I said about taking the time to educate a prospect and that the more complex or expensive the item or service, the more you must sell? Well, you are actually selling *yourself.* You are selling your expertise and you are giving your prospects a reason to trust you, your business, and the solutions that you bring them that solve their most challenging problems.

The late Chet Holmes taught us a script which is highly compelling which you should adopt at your seminar. At the beginning of the event, you should say,

"This entire seminar is 100% educational in nature and designed to serve you. I'm just going to take a little time at the end to tell you a bit about what's going on with us and how we might further serve you. Does that seem fair?"

And then you nod your head a little to evoke that response from the audience. In every case, people will nod with you and agree. So, what they've just done is given you their permission to sell to them later. When you slip in your sales pitch, they recognize it as such, but they aren't put off by it.

This is the essence of *permission-based marketing.* Permission-based marketing simply means that people give you the permission, *and often pay you,* to solicit them. Everyone has an area of expertise that others would be interested to know about.

You can use this in several different ways, depending on your situation and the complexity of your product or service.

If the information is valuable, you can even charge for it. But the key is this: *The information itself is not the product but leads the interested person to enter a buying relationship with you.* That means that you must have something else of value that they would desire to purchase on a one-time or on-going basis.

But here's the winning idea: *when you charge people to watch your valuable content, they are, in fact, paying you to solicit them.* And, they'll have no objection to it because they walk away with something of value whether they continue to buy from you or not.

Most businesses are too myopic to think of much else than making a single sale. In doing so, they limit any possible chance of being an industry leader and their growth will never go beyond linear.

There are six strategic objectives accomplished by a seminar:

1) You can establish your credibility.
2) You build trust and respect with your prospective clients.
3) You can impact people's lives.
4) You can get people to pay you to solicit them in a focused environment.

5) You can force yourself to express and articulate your viewpoints so that you have a more thorough knowledge of your material and the sales process.

6) You can record your material so that you can distribute your information in various formats.

That leads us to the next area where you can establish yourself as the expert:

Books, podcasts, video lessons, whitepapers, magazine articles (or article series), radio or TV shows, or newsletters.

Content is king, as they say. Take the time to make your content excellent. Study a lot! 10,000 hours is the new minimum. Knowledge is doubling every year (or faster)! Grow and specialize and outsource the actual medium of your content if you must. If you aren't adept at creating valuable content, find a content creator that can do the work for you.

Making it Practical

In your type of business, what are the 3 to 5 factors that build trust? Different businesses and people have different ways to build trust. Think about how you grow in your trust for another business.

- You read their educational content. It could be:
  - An E-book
  - Research report
  - An analyst reports
  - An expert guide
  - A comparison white paper (a white paper is just a report

that gives information on an issue)
- You watch them teach through:
  - A webinar
  - A video (or video series)
- You read their case studies of how others have solved problems that are similar to yours
- You read or watch testimonials from others who are singing their praises
- They give you a trial offer so you can dig in and see for yourself if the product or service lives up to your standard
- You see a comparison against their competitors
- You watch a live demonstration

All of these are trust building factors. And (if you've been paying attention) they are the same type of material that is required for each stage of the Buyer's Journey that we discussed in the last chapter.

However, there are even more ways that build trust:

1. Longevity in business which ties into reputation and a good name.
2. A recognizable brand.
3. A strong risk-reversal (E.g., "If you're not happy for any reason, bring it back within 30 days for a no-questions-asked refund.").
4. A recognizable partner or affiliated company (E.g., "We're a Microsoft partner.").
5. Quality marketing materials (website, brochures, business cards, etc.).

What type of information could/do you provide that leads people to the conclusion that they would be an absolute fool to do business with anyone but you?

How could you improve the way you communicate your benefits and expertise?

Do you have a supply of customer testimonials, success stories, or endorsements that are measurable?

Do you have a system in place for soliciting and capturing testimonials or success stories on an ongoing basis?

What would be the impact on *your* business if you created and followed a system to systematically capture and use testimonials or success stories or endorsements to build trust in your market?

This is the tip of the iceberg of questions you should be thinking about as you design and implement an expert-positioning strategy in your business.

This is also what I do. I live in this space and know the playing field very well.

How (the Boring Topic of) Policies and Procedures Can Dramatically Impact Your Profits

Policies and procedures aren't exciting and are rarely the latest trend but finding an impact in this area may simply be one of the easiest ways to see how you can optimize your profits very quickly without a major disruption to your current business.

The trouble with many entrepreneurs is that they become fed up with a job that "any robot can do". They then start their own business, not realizing that to become successful, they must create systems, policies, and procedures that allow the company to run in a way so that "any robot can do the job".

Let me first assume that you have weekly meetings with your staff. But if you're a solopreneur, then you still must set time aside each week to make decisions and create policies and procedures so that you're not always "flying by the seat of your pants".

When you make decisions in your weekly meetings, you must write down the decisions that are made and institute policies and procedures that employees and team members must follow. If these are written, then your current staff or incoming staff can easily reference them. This is why McDonald's restaurant is so streamlined and successful—they can get any new employee up to speed in a day because of great policies and procedures that are written and easy to follow.

Policies and procedures are what make your business run without you. It's the difference between the amateurs and the professionals.

Without policies and procedures, your business can never, ever maximize on all the opportunities with which you are presented. Furthermore, those businesses in your niche that are acting like professionals will sooner or later (and most likely sooner) eat you alive.

Here's one idea right now that explains a company policy that might work in your company culture. Each person in the business must write a "to do" list at the beginning of the month which they will divide into weekly action plans, which will end up as daily "to do" lists.

The policy or procedure of the supervisor is that he will inspect each monthly "to do" list, each weekly action plan, and each daily "to do" list. What do you think will happen to a worker's productivity if he or she knows that the boss is going to come every morning and inspect what they have planned for the day? How much greater would *your* focus be if you had someone holding you accountable for the way you spend your hours through the day? Normally, productivity will go up 20% overnight.

Companies that have remote workers (more common in a post-Covid society) can use online tracking systems such as TimeDoctor.

The supervisor gets a daily log of what hours the workers are spending on work-related tasks, what time is wasted, and even screenshots of what their employees are looking at through the day. If an employee doesn't want the boss to see what he was looking at, he can easily delete the screenshot, but it also deletes the corresponding hours.

Oversight like this works for *some* company cultures. In other cultures, it may demotivate your workforce because they don't want that type of oversight. It can also depend on the type of role your employee plays. Creative roles operate differently than regular task-based roles and their jobs may require them to spend time consuming all types of content including time spent on YouTube. You must be sensitive to the responses of your employees how you bring oversight to your company.

Another example of a policy would be specifically for your sales force. Some studies have shown that 80% of sales are made after the fifth call. However,

- 48% of salespeople call once and give up.
- 25% call twice and quit.
- 12% make three calls and stop.
- 5% give up after the fourth call.
- Only 10% keep calling. 10% makes 80% of the sales.

Do you have a company culture that allows a salesperson to do whatever they want, based on the mood they're in that day? Or do you have a policy that they must try at least five times – and do you inspect what they have done and hold them to consequences if they don't do what they are supposed to?

Perhaps in your business niche, it takes, on average, at least seven attempts to get an appointment with a prospect. If your salesperson gives up after the second or third attempt, and they aren't following up at least seven times, you're not going to make the sale. But you must have policies and procedures laid out, and you must monitor them, so you know that your salesperson has (for example),

1. first sent a card,
2. then telephoned,
3. then sent a letter,
4. then an email,
5. then another call,
6. then a visit,
7. then a call,
8. Etc.

You should know what period is between each action, and you can see the results. However, if you have no policies, plans, and procedures, you're just letting your sales staff do whatever they want and then you're lucky to get anything at all.

Creating policies and procedures is hard work – it takes time to type out policies and monitor them so that everyone does what they are supposed to. But this is the key to running a great company and this is the key to great marketing. You need to focus on this too if you want a great company that keeps running even when you're off on holiday!

Most small business owners have zero to few written policies. You can almost always find an impact here in your business.

What if you knew that you would grow so fast that you had to hire one new person every day for the next six months, and that this trend would start in 30 days? Basically, you'd have one month to get ready, and you'd want your business to hum along at high speed without getting bogged down by newcomers who fumbled around not knowing what to do.

If you're not growing at a rapid pace right now, what better time is there than *now* to create these policies and procedures. You certainly don't want to be caught without the time.

Better two years too early than one day too late!

Here's your other caveat: If your employees need to ask a question, they should be able to answer the question by looking in the company manual (which could easily be an online reference guide that is accessible from any place). What would you put in the manual? What should you at least consider?

Sales & Marketing Processes

1. **Lead Generation**
   a) Creation and use of brochures, promotional pieces, and other corporate literature
   b) Email
   c) Advertising
   d) The Internet (including website building and maintenance, funnel building, lead capture, monitoring metrics, etc.)
   e) Article writing and publishing
   f) Public Relations
   g) Multiple referral systems
   h) Social media engagement
   i) Personal contact (sales, customer service)
   j) Seminars, trade shows

2. **Lead Conversion**
   a) Follow-up
   b) Contracts
   c) Metrics and reporting
   d) Onboarding process

3. **Sales Management**
   a) Expectation and accountability
   b) Training

c) Communication

d) Use of tools

A company is deemed to be more valuable if it has documented sales and marketing processes and procedures so that *sales are predictable.*

Operations Processes

1. Increasing customer satisfaction
2. Handling customer complaints
3. Handling new customers
4. Processing refund requests

Management Processes

1. Recruiting and Interviews
2. Answering the phone
3. Employee Handbook/Manual
4. New Employee Training Plan
5. Existing Employee Training Plan and Skill Development
6. Finance and Accounting (budgeting, statements, reporting, etc.)
7. Collections
8. Meetings
9. Performance Reviews
10. Workflow and work management
11. Expectations, goals, and plans for employee productivity

12. Employee Discipline

13. Time Management

Making it Practical

What processes, procedures, and policies do you currently have that are written down and accessible to relevant staff?

If you incorporated policies/ procedures/ rewards/ consequences for your staff to follow, and you followed through on them, what impact would that have on your business?

We start with these numbers as our motivation to implement the changes that are necessary. When you see that implementation of an action should bring you $40,000 (for example) over the course of a year, then you'll be more highly motivated to act.

You won't see this impact immediately but don't get discouraged. It will all start to accumulate in an exponential manner.

Next, you're going to have a lot of areas where you'll need to see policies and procedures implemented. But if you try to do everything at once, you'll get overwhelmed and possibly end up implementing nothing, or just a few things poorly. For that reason, you'll need to choose a few areas where you can test the new positioning immediately.

What are the three greatest areas of impact that, if you had excellent procedures and policies, you would see a significant impact in the way your business functions and grows?

What are the three greatest areas of impact that, if you had excellent procedures and policies, you would see a significant impact in the *long term* in the way your business functions and grows?

What one area will you be willing to implement in the next week that will have the greatest immediate impact? (E.g., If it is culturally acceptable, having employees write out their daily list of work to accomplish, and the manager will check it at the start of the day and the end of the day—this should boost productivity immediately.)

The more specific that you can be with implementation details, the more likely you are to succeed. How will you easily implement your new policies and procedures in a way that will cause the least disruption to your current business, but will have the greatest impact?

1) Who will be the responsible person in your organization?
2) What priorities will you set?
3) What start dates will are appropriate?
4) What completion dates are appropriate?
5) What resources do they need to accomplish their goal?
6) What system will you use to build your Policies and Procedures which can be easily accessed at appropriate levels by any staff?
7) What are the benefits to the responsible person if they accomplish this goal?

8) What are the consequences if they fail in this?

9) What challenges stand in your way?

10) What can you do to overcome these challenges?

11) What are you willing to commit to?

12) How will you train your staff to follow the best methods you create?

You, see? We'll leave no stone unturned.

How To Write Persuasive Marketing
Part 1

In this chapter, I'm going to teach you the secrets to persuasive marketing, and how you can use it to influence your prospects to buy what you sell. The business owner who understands how to create messages, ads, and marketing collateral that follows a persuasion format can literally gain the ability to dominate their market.

And because of the critical nature of this information, this information will be delivered in two chapters.

Part 1 will focus on understanding the fundamentals of human nature and part 2 will focus on the actual persuasion elements required for effective marketing.

Persuasion Marketing is simply organizing the buying and selling processes so you can present compelling information about your product or service that will persuade your prospects to take a specific action. All marketing should inform and persuade your prospects.

With Persuasion Marketing, you strive to be successful in addressing the wants and needs of all prospects in such a way that you continue to move them through their various stages of decision making.

The problem is that today, these so-called "marketing experts" are teaching business owners all sorts of tips, tricks, tools, and gimmicks designed to help them convert a prospect into a client. But here's the problem. Most of them no longer work. Prospects have "wised-up" to the trickery. They have become jaded, skeptical, and distrustful.

That's not to say that exclusivity and scarcity no longer work; they just no longer work using the same tired tactics that have been employed for years. Smart business owners must start thinking outside the box.

This chapter is going to teach you how to market the correct way by giving you a process that proves to your prospects that your business, and your business alone, provides the ultimate value for the price your prospects pay.

For example, several large surveys show that most people believe a logical discussion, coupled with good data and the right logical supporting facts, are the best ways to persuade a prospect to buy what you sell.

But we learned that following this process is one sure-fire way to fail at persuasion. Why? Neuroscientists have recently discovered that the brain waves we emit when we engage in logical thinking are virtually identical to those we emit when we're forced to plunge our hands and arms into ice water. It's painful!

Furthermore, these researchers have determined that our brains require 300 percent more effort—measured in calories burned—for heavy thinking, compared with "mental cruising."

No wonder people hate a logical, reasoned approach! Luckily for us, our brains are hard-wired with mechanisms that help us make good decisions without painstaking analysis and reasoning. These mechanisms are known as triggers, but you can also think of them as "hot buttons." Essentially, they're the decision-making shortcuts we easily and naturally employ all day long. They are our automatic self-guidance systems. We often don't even realize we're using them!

Put simply, hot buttons are our navigational aids. They help us make easy, non-analytical, yet correct decisions. There are seven major persuasion elements we all depend on to help us easily make quick, automatic, and right decisions.

Let's discuss these fundamentals. It's critical that you commit these to memory and remember them for the rest of your life as a business owner. They're based on fundamental human nature and will be as applicable 500 years from now as they were 500 years ago.

Fundamental #1 – Everyone wants the "best deal".

Your prospects, no matter who they are or what it is they're buying, always want the best deal. That doesn't mean the lowest price; it means the most value for the price they pay. They will gladly pay twice the price *if* they perceive they're receiving four times the value when they compare it to the price.

The key words here of course are "perceived value". What exactly do prospects value? They value finding the solution to their biggest problem, frustration, fear, or concern. And that brings us to...

Fundamental #2 – Always market to the negative.

Never forget that the vast majority of human beings will do anything to avoid pain, but very little to gain pleasure.

One of the biggest mistakes I see business owners make every day is they try to market to the positive and avoid the negative like the plague. That's the worst thing they can possibly do.

Prospects don't want to lose weight to feel better and regain their health. They want to lose weight because their doctor told them if they don't, they won't live another five years, or they hate the way they look, or the way they're treated, or the fact that their self-esteem has been damaged.

Show them the solution to these so-called "hot button" issues and they will buy from you forever.

Fundamental #3 – Prospects buy based on emotion.

This is a big one. People make buying decisions based mostly on emotion. They mainly use logic to justify their purchase. This ties in directly with marketing to the negative. Prospects either want out of pain or they want to avoid pain, and that resonates with them emotionally.

If you were a child psychologist who specialized in helping parents with emotionally disturbed and out-of-control kids, which of the following headlines in an ad would immediately grab your ideal prospect's attention?

"I can help you rediscover the joy and happiness your family deserves."

Or,

"Would you like a 5-minute solution that will end the yelling, screaming and belligerent attitude of your child forever?"

That's kind of a no-brainer, isn't it? Market to the negative and make it as emotionally compelling as possible. Hit your prospects squarely in their hot buttons, and you automatically make an emotional connection.

Fundamental #4 – Make your business "unique".

One of the biggest problems business owners face when trying to make that emotional connection is that different prospects have different hot buttons. That's why it's critical that you separate your business from your competition. You must find a way to stand out from the crowd. The best way to do this is to create a "niche" market for your business. That means your business must stop trying to be everything to everyone.

If you were a left-handed golfer with a horrendous slice, and you decided to seek professional help to improve your golf game, who would you call? The professional with the ad in the paper that says

I help golfers improve their golf game.

Or the pro with the ad that says,

I help left-handed golfers with horrendous slices get rid of their slice permanently within 3 days or you don't pay.

That's what we call a "niche" market, and you will attract every prospect within that niche because you offer what they specifically *want*. When you try to be everything to everyone, you're nothing to no one. When you select a niche market, a niche based on your passion for what you do, you instantly become "unique", since your competition is trying to be all things to all people.

Prospects are looking for the expert. They demand the best. Positioning your business into its own niche market positions you as that expert. It's a concept known as pre-eminence, and it begins to create value for what you do. And speaking of value,

Fundamental #5 – Create "extraordinary value".

Would I shock you if I told you that your prospects could care less about price? They shop price because they're forced to. Let me explain. What prospects really want is the best *value* for the price they pay. They're more than willing to pay double the price if they perceive that you're giving them four times the value. Now they know they're getting the "best deal".

So then why does price seem to matter so often? It's because so few businesses are actually "unique". They all look the same, and they all say the exact same things. They say things like "*we're the best, we have the lowest prices, the highest quality, the best selection, the most*

43

convenient hours and locations and we've been in business since 1431 B.C."

We call these platitudes, and they mean absolutely nothing to your prospects. That's because everything just mentioned was about the business, and your prospects don't care one bit about your business. All prospects care about is themselves. They want to know how they will benefit from what you sell. How will their life improve if they purchase your product or service?

If what you sell solves a problem in their life, or if it removes a major frustration, fear, or concern, then they see your product or service as "valuable". Again, we call these problems, frustrations, fears, and concerns "hot buttons".

After you select your niche market, you must find out what the "hot buttons" are for that niche market. And then ask yourself openly and honestly if your business offers a solution for those hot buttons. If you don't, you need to "innovate" and create a solution. If you do offer a solution, is it unique? Meaning, is it really different from your competition and does it offer extraordinary value? Or is it the exact same solution your competition offers?

If it is, then you and your competition are doomed to forever compete on price. You must *innovate* your business to create a unique, extraordinary solution that separates your business from all competitors. You see, there's no magic involved in selling. All you

44

must do is find out what your prospects really "want" and then give it to them.

Your job as the business owner is to make sure your business offers them exactly what they want, and that means positioning yourself in a niche market and then innovating your business to give that niche exactly what they're looking for. That creates "extraordinary value".

Fundamental #6 – Be able to communicate your uniqueness and extraordinary value.

You must create a highly targeted, laser-focused message aimed specifically at the prospects in your niche market so you can tell them you have exactly what they want. We refer to this message as your "elevator pitch". It's basically a ten- to thirty-second mini-commercial for your business.

That pitch must highlight the way you overcome their hot buttons in a unique way that offers extraordinary value. When you communicate your elevator pitch to a prospect and they respond by saying, "How do you do that?" then you know you have a terrific elevator pitch.

Fundamental #7 – Prospects buy what they want, not what they need.

This is another big one to never forget. This ties back to the fact that prospects buy based on emotion and they only use logic to justify their purchase. When you *need* something, you are drawing a logical

45

conclusion. The problem is this. Prospects may or may not buy what they *need* but they more often buy what they *want*. Whereas needs are based on logic, "wants" are based on emotion. Here is an example.

You look at your 3-year-old car and notice the tires are almost worn slick. So logically you say to yourself, "Oh no. I need new tires. Oh heck, they'll last a few more months." Even though you need new tires, you don't want them. Why? They're not cheap to replace, it's inconvenient for you to take the time to hunt for the best deal on tires, then you must make an appointment to have them changed, and then there's the inconvenience of having to have it done while you wait two hours for the work to be completed. In short, it's a hassle.

Now consider this scenario. You just purchased a brand-new car and as you're leaving the dealership, you see the same car you just bought with a new style of tire on it that really complements the car. In fact, it significantly enhances the beauty of the car. You *want* those tires.

Even though they're twice as expensive as the ones you have already purchased, and the hassle factor is the same as the first scenario, you *want* those tires and so you will have them. The first situation involved logic and the second situation involved emotion. So never forget that prospects buy what they want, not what they need. It all goes back to emotion.

If you can create marketing messages that hit these major fundamentals, you will absolutely dominate your competition.

So as a quick review. The seven fundamental human behaviors to focus on that will help you create persuasive marketing are:

- Fundamental #1 – Everyone wants the "best deal".

- Fundamental #2 – Always market to the negative.

- Fundamental #3 – Prospects buy based on emotion.

- Fundamental #4 – Make your business "unique".

- Fundamental #5 – Create "extraordinary value".

  - Fundamental #6 – Be able to communicate your uniqueness and extraordinary value.

  - Fundamental #7 – Prospects buy what they want, not what they need.

So how do you use these fundamentals to create persuasive marketing? To make this simple, remember this one important fact. Marketing is a science. And like everything in science, there's a very simple equation that, when followed, will always produce the right result. That equation is known as the *Conversion Equation.*

In the next chapter, we're going to go in-depth and thoroughly explore the Conversion Equation. This will establish a persuasion format that you will be able to follow for the rest of your life as a small business owner, and when you do, you will literally be able to dominate your competition.

How To Write Persuasive Marketing
Part 2

In the previous chapter, we discussed the importance of creating a compelling message. In this chapter, we're going to go in-depth and thoroughly explore the *Conversion Equation*. This will establish a persuasion format that you will be able to follow for the rest of your life as a small business owner, and when you do, you will literally be able to dominate your competition.

The Conversion Equation can be broken down into four basic components:

Interrupt, Engage, Educate and **Offer**. It's based on one of the oldest and most durable models known because it helps business owners appeal to consumers' emotional and social wants and needs. Let me explain why this equation is so important for business owners to fully understand.

For your marketing message to be effective, you must sharpen the focus of your message to ensure that you reach your prospect's mind and that you do so with enough impact that he or she will pick up the phone, walk into the store, or go to the web site and get involved with your business.

But here's the problem: Your prospects are swimming, drowning, suffocating in marketing messages. We all are. Today, we live in a media-saturated world where we're endlessly exposed to a constant barrage of advertising messages from the moment, we wake up to the time we go to bed.

Because they're inundated with marketing messages, your prospects will filter most of these messages right out of their conscious thought— unless one happens to hit them squarely on their hot button.

You must put time and effort into investigating exactly who your prospects are, what their most pressing want is, and how your business fulfils that want.

That's why you always begin with a Target Customer Profile or Customer Avatar and then understand their thought process.

Once you know who is buying what you sell and how they decide to buy, your marketing message must hit a resounding bull's-eye on your target customer's hot button by using a highly targeted and strategically placed message that will compel him or her to buy, or at least, to take the next step.

For any type of marketing to work, it *must* do three things. It *must* grab the reader's attention, it *must* facilitate the prospect's information gathering & decision-making process, and it *must* provide a specific, low risk, easy to take action that helps them make a good decision. Why are these three steps so important? Let's go through them.

First, all marketing must grab the prospect's attention. If it doesn't, it's worthless. They'll never read, watch, or listen to the rest of your ad. That means you must have a great headline if the ad is in print. If it's on the radio, the headline is the first thing they hear. If it's on TV, the headline is the first thing they see and hear.

Second, we just discussed that every prospect, no matter who they are or what they buy, is always looking for the best deal. That doesn't mean the lowest price; it means the most value for the price they pay. To know if something is the best deal, they must have decision-making information.

Your marketing *must* help the prospect gather information that aids them in their decision-making process. That's why you must develop a client profile and map out your prospect's thought process. Without these fundamentals in place, you won't know the right information to provide them with.

And third, your marketing must contain a low or, better yet, no risk offer to further facilitate the prospect's decision-making process. You must give them a compelling, yet safe way to take the next step. Note that this "next step" may not necessarily be to plunk down their credit card then and there and buy your product or service.

It may be to pick up the phone to make an appointment so they can learn more, to order a free trial, or to visit a retail location. Whatever it is, what you want is a concrete action step that gets your prospect actively involved with your business. These three principles must always be present if your marketing is going to be effective.

Now, to help ensure that you always include these three principles, all you need to do is follow the Conversion Equation for every marketing piece you develop. Remember, the Conversion Equation goes like this: Interrupt, Engage, Educate and Offer.

Let me explain these more in depth. You must first **Interrupt** your prospects. In other words, you must gain their attention. This is done with an attention-grabbing headline. The headline is by far the single most important part of any ad. If your prospects don't read the headline, then they won't read the rest of the ad, no matter how well it is written. If your headline doesn't do its job, the rest of the project is nothing but a waste of time, effort, and money.

In a print piece, the headline is placed at the very top of the ad. Most businesses place the name of their company here, and again, that is the worst thing you can ever do. Your prospects don't care one iota what you have named your business. They don't care what you look like either, so stop putting your picture at the top as well.

Make that headline hot button-oriented and if the ad is a print ad, be sure the headline is in the largest type, so the eye goes to it first. If you use a radio ad, the headline is the first thing the listener hears, so hit those listeners in their emotional hot buttons.

If it's written correctly, the right attention-grabbing headline also serves a second crucial function that many marketers and business owners don't think about. It immediately qualifies your target customer and disqualifies those prospects who aren't your target customer. A well-written headline will only grab the attention of those prospects who genuinely want your product or service—and they're the only ones you want to grab, right?

When you create your Target Customer Profile, you will know exactly what your target customer wants. When you map out your target customer's thought process, then you further refine and focus on those wants by specifically defining their hot buttons and creating the innovations your business must have to dominate your market. All of this gives you the raw material you need to draw on for your headlines.

Now you've grabbed your prospect's attention; that's the good news. Here's the bad news: You only have it for two to three seconds. Remember that your client lives in a world of media overwhelm. Simply grabbing their attention is not going to get your message across because the moment after you've grabbed it, it's gone ... unless you're carefully following our cut-through-the-clutter Conversion Equation.

Once you've grabbed your prospect's attention, you must ensure that the very next thing they read **engages** that attention, and this is the sub-headline's job. Think of the headline like you're tapping on a glass with your spoon at a dinner party to get everyone's attention so you can give a toast. The sub-headline would be the first line you speak when you start giving the toast.

Your sub-headline needs to engage your prospect's attention by persuasively promising to provide them with vital decision-making information that will solve their major problem, frustration, fear, or concern. In other words, your sub-headline builds on the impact of the headline and fleshes it out with enough specifics to make it sufficiently intriguing that the reader will want to read further.

Your sub-headline should be in the second-largest font in your marketing piece, plus it should be placed directly below, or immediately after your headline, so there's no ambiguity whatsoever. Your reader's eye now knows exactly where to go.

The headline and sub-headline work together to Interrupt and Engage your target customer by promising to provide them with vital, decision-making information that will solve their major concern or frustration.

Please note that the Interrupt and Engage components are two of the most important marketing fundamentals that, when mastered, can have a tremendous impact on your marketing results, and immediately help you to attract more clients.

You *must* properly structure your headline to hit your prospect's hot buttons, and structure the sub-headline to indicate the ad contains the solution to the problem the headline addresses.

So just remember that when you create any type of marketing message, you want to Interrupt and Engage your prospects with an attention-grabbing headline, followed by a sub-headline that promises a solution to the problem referenced in the headline.

Next, you want to **Educate** your reader by providing them with significant information about how it is that your business delivers on the promise of the headline and sub-headline. This is the task of the lengthiest piece of text in your entire marketing piece, which is the body copy.

In your body copy, make sure you emphasize the benefits the prospect wants and not simply the features you have. The single biggest and most common mistake business owners make is to focus constantly on their business's features, and not on its benefits. *Features tell, benefits sell.*

Businesses that focus on features are doomed to forever compete on price. Businesses that focus on benefits always compete on value.

It's important to remember that every prospect is looking for the best deal. Therefore, it's imperative that your body copy informs your prospects about the extraordinary value you offer with crystal clarity.

Most of the time, you will need to innovate your business to *create*, and then *offer* extraordinary value.

Focusing on your innovations is the key to marketing success. You *must* create value; that is what your prospects are looking for. And innovation is the way to create massive, extraordinary value.

While the body copy is by far the longest portion of the ad, this is still a marketing piece, not an informational pamphlet, brochure, or catalog. Resist the temptation to throw in every bit of juicy information you can think of and remember to focus on only one hot button at a time. You want to give them just enough information to entice them to want to know even more.

Although you have now successfully grabbed and held your prospect's attention, remember that the rest of the media-saturated world is still there clamoring to be heard. You only have a minute or two to inform your prospect as to how your product or service will benefit them.

Benefits sell, features tell. Always highlight the benefits of your innovations. Now put all this information into the body copy of your ad so that you fully educate your prospects.

And finally, you must always end your marketing message with a compelling **Offer**. Whether it's a postcard, a direct sales letter, a print ad, a television or radio commercial, a live event, a web page—no matter what form or format you use, every piece needs to close with a compelling offer.

If you don't, ninety-nine prospects out of a hundred will simply walk away. Your prospect will not take any action unless you ask them to do so and give them a very good reason why they should do so.

Your offer has one purpose and one purpose only—to get your prospect to take a specific action. That's why the offer is often referred to as the "call to action". Your compelling offer needs to be a low- or better yet no-risk way to lead your prospect to take the next step in your sales process.

This is persuasive marketing and as you can see, it's a process, *not* an event. Your competition is treating it as an event. They send out a postcard or build a website and then sit back and wonder why their phone isn't ringing or no one is visiting their website. There's simply more to marketing these days than just "getting your name out there."

You now know the process and you have the marketing equation to guide you through it. If you act on this information, you should see a dramatic increase in the number of leads you begin to generate, the number of clients you begin to attract, and the amount of money you see accumulating on your bottom line.

I can also promise you this. Your competition isn't doing any of this. If you act right now, you will position yourself and your business far ahead of the curve. They won't know what has hit them. You will be positioning your business as the obvious choice for any prospect to do business with.

You will set your business up as the premier dominant force in your industry and virtually no one will be able to compete with you again. You will simply offer so much additional value that, even if you charge substantially more than your competition, your value will supersede the price and make buying from you a foregone conclusion.

5 Key Marketing Components That Will Ruin Your Competition
Part 1

This chapter will focus on teaching you the 5 key marketing components that will ruin your competition. Because this chapter contains a tremendous number of important concepts and accompanying content, this will be Part 1.

In this chapter, I'll teach you the 5 components and show you how they all work together to produce amazing financial results for you, once you understand how to use them. Then in part two, I'll show you an actual marketing campaign that was implemented years ago where the marketing was based solely on the implementation of these 5 marketing components.

I mention many times through this book that marketing depends on your ability to establish trust, respect, and rapport.

You won't establish any of these if you can't convey the fact that you're credible.

The 5 key marketing components that will ruin your competition are also the 5 components that will establish your credibility with your prospects.

The 5 components are:

1. The Ignition Code,
2. Drawing a line in the sand,
3. Using powerful language,
4. Social proof,
5. Evidence.

We're going to spend much of the time talking about #2 and #3 – drawing a line in the sand and using powerful language. But let me start by explaining what I meant when I said the first component is the "ignition code".

The "ignition code" comes from a movie called "The Transporter," featuring Jason Statham. Jason is a major action star and was also featured in the movie Expendables 2. I want to encourage you to watch The Transporter. Watch the first 10 minutes of the movie and you will see the actual scene that features the ignition code. But for now, let me briefly explain what happens and what I want you to take away from the first scene in this movie.

At the very beginning of this film, you've got Jason's character sitting in a parking garage in a BMW 7-Series wearing a black suit.

An alarm goes off on his watch, so he turns on some classical music and puts on a pair of black leather gloves.

Then you see him driving through the city. The location is somewhere in France, perhaps along the Mediterranean. At this point, we have no idea who he is or what he's doing, but he eventually pulls up in front of what appears to be a bank. As he pulls up, stops, and turns off his car's engine, you see the clock in the bank's bell tower indicate it's the top of the hour, and immediately 4 masked gunmen come storming out of the bank holding bags of money. They're obviously robbing this bank, and the guy in the car is the getaway driver.

As the gunmen pile into the car, the lead robber turns to the driver and says, "Get us out of here!" The driver doesn't move; he just sits there staring straight ahead. The lead robber yells at him to "get going!" Again, no response. Finally, the driver turns to look at the lead robber and says, "Rule #1, never change the deal. The deal was 3 men, 276 kilograms. There are 4 of you!"

The lead robber screams, "Who cares? Let's go!" Again, the driver repeats his previous statement, and then he explains how his car has just enough fuel for 3 guys at 276 kilograms, how the shocks on his car are adjusted for 3 guys at 276 kilograms.

"With 4 guys, our chances of getting caught by the police go up exponentially." Then he says, "I don't want to get caught. Do you want to get caught?"

The lead robber places his gun to the driver's head and, as he does, one of the robbers in the back seat yells out, "Shoot this idiot and I'll drive the car!"

The driver, as cool and calm as ever, merely turns his head toward the robber holding the gun and softly says, "Not without the ignition code, you won't."

Now here's the point to this scene in this movie. When someone is holding a gun to your head, you automatically assume that individual has all the power in that situation.

But when the robbers realized the car wasn't running, and that this specific BMW required the entry of an ignition code to start the car, the power shifted to the driver. The lead robber had no choice. He turned toward the back seat and shot one of his own men. The others pushed him out of the car and the driver casually said, "Seat belts everyone" and off they went.

Now apply this same principle to a business environment.

As a business owner, it's critical that you develop an ignition code for your business so that we can switch the power from your customer, from your prospect, back over to you as the business owner.

In your business, do you have an ignition code?

An ignition code simply refers to your market-dominating position.

It means that no matter what you do, whatever your business, your competition can't touch you. You simply offer more value than anyone else in your industry. A prospect would be an absolute fool if they bought what you sell from anyone else but you, period! That's an ignition code.

Former President Lyndon B. Johnson may have said it best years ago:

"What convinces is conviction.

Believe in the argument you're advancing.

If you don't, you're as good as dead.

The other person will sense that something isn't there, and no chain of reasoning, no matter how logical or elegant or brilliant will win your case for you."

When you have an ignition code, you automatically gain confidence as well, just like the driver in The Transporter did. He knew he held all the power, and even though he wasn't armed and the other 4 guys in the car all were, he held all the power, and they were literally helpless to do anything about it.

Confidence comes from having an "ignition code". And confidence is what customers and prospects are looking for from the businesses they transact with. So, let's find out if you have an ignition code. And to know for sure, I want you to think in terms of our other marketing methodologies. Remember that there are three basic fundamentals that make up great marketing.

- Have something good to say
- Say it well
- Say it often.

Your ignition code is when you have something good to say. There is actually a term that's used to describe this. It's called moral ascendancy, which means that I know that I'm the best person to get this job done.

Think about some of the greats in the history of sports. Michael Jordan is arguably the greatest basketball player to have ever played the game. He knew that at any given moment when he stepped foot onto the basketball court; he was going to dominate the other team. He didn't wonder. He didn't hope. He *knew* and it led him to win pretty much everything every year.

Tiger Woods in his heyday was the same way. LeBron James may be in this category. But this doesn't just apply to sports, it applies to business as well.

When you walk into the home of your customer, if you have an in-home sales appointment, do you absolutely, positively, 100% know that you're the best option when it comes to buying what you sell?

When you're talking to people on the phone, or when you send out any form of marketing collateral, are you communicating that fact to your prospects?

That's why I keep saying repeatedly that you *must* have a market dominating position for your business. And if you don't have a market dominating position, if you don't have your own ignition code, that's when you *must* stop right where you are and innovate your business, so you do have one.

You will never have your own ignition code until you believe in your own heart that you offer the best solution for your prospects.

What do you do that is quantifiably better than anyone else?

What could you do to innovate your own business that would give you an ignition code advantage? In The Transporter, the driver had a definitive advantage in that relationship. He held all the power. The robbers had to deal with him on his terms because he was the only one that possessed that ignition code. Do you feel like that in your business? Can you look your prospects in the eye and say, "You can do business with whomever you want? You can give your money to anyone you want. I could honestly care less, because I know that if you don't give it to me, then you're going to get a raw deal."

This transitions into the next two principles I mentioned earlier - *drawing a line in the sand* and *powerful language.* Once you have an ignition code, then it's time to draw the line in the sand. Let me give you my take on this from the standpoint of a real-life business consultant.

This consultant had a client that was multimillion dollar company in Toronto, Canada. They asked him to meet with them about a new marketing campaign they were launching. They were preparing to send out 20,000 postcards to a targeted list of qualified prospects—a list they had purchased from a reputable list broker. OK, so far so good. Then they showed him the postcard they were sending out. It was the exact same worthless, platitude-filled junk that most businesses send out these days.

The postcard basically said, "Hey, we're pretty good at what we do so why aren't you doing business with us?" Seriously, that was the gist (or jest) of this entire postcard. The two owners showed him this postcard and asked him for his professional opinion. The consultant asked them if there was any way humanly possible, they could stop the postcards from being mailed. They said they couldn't—that the mail house already had all 20,000 of them and they were going out the following day. Then they asked him why he was so concerned.

He had to level with them that, in his professional opinion, they wouldn't receive so much as a single phone call.

He then took the postcard and explained to them in detail why it wouldn't work and how he would have redesigned it. By the time he was finished, one of the partners was absolutely steaming.

He told the consultant that he was nuts, especially if he thought for one minute that sending out 20,000 targeted postcards wouldn't result in a single phone call. They basically concluded the meeting at that point and showed him the door.

Two weeks later they called him and apologized. Turns out they didn't receive a single phone call and asked him to take over their marketing campaign for them.

Now why did the consultant remain so steadfast in his dealings with this company? After all, wouldn't it have been easier to just placate the clients and tell them what they wanted to hear?

Well, not when you have the ignition code you don't. The consultant knew that his marketing methodology worked and knew the results they were going to get.

Placating them would have only served to tarnish his professional reputation, not enhance his stature with them. In fact, had he agreed that their marketing collateral was OK, it would have damaged any chance for a future relationship with this company. But notice what the consultant did there.

He knew he had the ignition code and that allowed him to draw a line in the sand and tell them they weren't going to get any business after spending a lot of money on this futile campaign. The postcards didn't contain powerful language. Instead, it was full of worthless platitudes that failed to establish confidence and certainty in their prospects.

So again, when you look at your business, what is your ignition code?

Do you have an ignition code advantage? Because once you do, it's time to draw a line in the sand. So, let's talk about drawing a line in the sand. There's an old adage that says, "You can't be everything to everyone," and that's absolutely 100% true.

You must decide what you want to be, who you want to serve, and then you must carve out that niche and forget about everyone else. So, what's your niche? What do you do? Who are you?

You need to decide what you want to be, and you've got to develop that niche and avoid everything else. When you do, you're going to build a lot of credibility with that relatively small group of prospects. How small? It doesn't matter. Just so long as it's big enough to support what you're trying to accomplish financially.

You *must* draw a line in the sand.

You've must decide what you are versus what you are not.

What do you stand for?

What are you? And don't try to be all things to all people. It's about finding your prospect's hottest hot button.

Which hot buttons are the most important to your customer?

Which hot buttons do you have a natural ability to service? At which you can excel?

Around which ones could you most easily innovate your business?

And here's what we're really trying to discover. What's your hottest hot button?

What one hot button could you really excel at? Now, I'm going to give you several examples of this in part two of the next chapter, so hang in there. It will all come together shortly. But here's what I want you to think about right now. I talked about the ignition code. This is really an extension of that discussion. You see, I want to create a position for you in the customer's mind.

I want your prospects and customers to look at you and say, "Okay, I get it. Here's what they do."

So, you *must* choose your prospect's hottest hot button and draw a line in the sand.

That line represents what you're going to be known for.

You're establishing your market-dominating position. So let me ask you this. Right now, this very minute, what are you known for?

If someone looked at your current marketing collateral or your website and they've never heard of you before, would it be obvious to them what you stand for? Or would your marketing look just like everyone else's these days? Full of platitudes and vagueness that attempts to be all things to all people?

It's this vagueness that brings us to our third component—using powerful language.

When you speak with power, people believe you are powerful.
When you speak with power, people are drawn to you.
When you speak with power, your character and competency aren't questioned.
When people talk tough, when people talk bold, when people talk with power, they tend to possess that power. Think about one of the

greatest talkers of all time, Mohammad Ali. What a great talker Mohammad Ali was. He let his opponents know in the press conference that it was all over before he ever stepped foot in the ring, and that was part of his persona. Now you may be thinking that I'm referring to intimidation here or being arrogant and cocky.

Not at all. What I'm talking about is standing for something, drawing a line in the sand, and then using powerful language that communicates that exact position. When you speak with power, you stand out from the crowd. Why? Because no one else does it.

You see commercials on TV every day, you hear them on the radio, you see them when you're online. They either don't know how to communicate powerfully, or they don't have anything worthwhile to say, so when you speak with power and you can back it up with a market-dominating position, then you're going to stand out from everyone else just by the way you talk.

So, let me give you the principles behind Power Talk. There are 11 of them.

Power Talk Principle #1: Be specific.

The more detail you convey, the more credible you become. Think of all the times you have heard someone say that "*we provide the best customer service*". That's a vague platitude that means nothing to most prospects. But suppose I'm a doctor, and in my ad, I say, " *We provide the best customer service in the medical community. When you show up for your appointment, your wait time to see the doctor will be less than 5 minutes, guaranteed!"* See the difference? Be specific.

Power Talk Principle #2: Acknowledge the concerns of your prospects.

This goes back to the hot buttons I mentioned earlier. Most people are extremely busy today, so visiting the doctor and having to wait an hour or more to be seen is usually a major concern for most patients. Therefore, acknowledge that hot button issue right from the start.

Power Talk Principle #3: Tell the story if and when it's appropriate.

In this case, the story is the case you make to support your market dominating position. I'll show you examples of this shortly.

Power Talk Principle #4: Have a strong opinion.

This one may be the most important point of them all. Guess what people want when they go to buy something? They want a strong opinion. Suppose you owned a store that specialized in selling vacuum cleaners. Your competitive situation is typical. You're competing with the likes of Costco, Target, and Walmart, and they're all selling crummy, low-cost vacuums that's taking business from you. However, *you're* the expert in this town when it comes to vacuums.

Now remember what I said people want. They want to talk to someone that has a strong opinion. Most sales people simply ask a prospect what they're looking for. Most prospects have *no* idea what to look for, especially when it comes to vacuums. What you want to do first is ask about their specific situation. Then we want to tell them what they specifically need. After all, how many times does a prospect get the opportunity to speak with a vacuum cleaner expert? I guarantee you this, if you go down to Target, Costco, Walmart, or Sam's Club, you aren't going to be talking to an expert. You're going to be talking to a teenager who at best has been schooled to regurgitate a series of talking points that explain nothing more than the basic features of the device.

When you voice a strong opinion, you stand out from everyone else. But understand this, when people go to buy something, they want confidence that they're buying the right thing that will produce the end result they're looking for.

They want confidence that they're getting the best deal, which means the most value for the price they pay.

A strong opinion gives them that confidence and they want you to have one.

People today don't want 50 different choices.

They want the best value for what will give them their desired result.

That's why I'm a big proponent of fewer choices.

I'm a huge proponent of just telling people what they need and backing that up with my strong opinion as to why I believe my recommendation is the best one for them, supported of course, by facts. Let me give you an example of this using the vacuum salesperson example. Let's say a young couple comes in looking for a vacuum.

If I do my job right, I must first analyze their exact situation.

I would want to find out

- What their budget is.
- What their specific carpet or flooring situation is.
- All the facts I need to make the proper recommendation.

Once I do that, here's how the conversation might go. And by the way, listen to the power language I use here. Listen to how I sell, by telling a story. And listen to the specifics I use to back up my strong opinion.

"OK, based on your current needs, here's my personal recommendation.

"First, did you know that there are 52 different brands of vacuum cleaners? We've evaluated all 52 of them for you. We found that out of 52, 44 of them weren't fit to be sold. They were cheap and inexpensively manufactured. They break easily. They don't have adequate suction

power. They don't last long, so we immediately eliminated them from our showroom.

"If you like, we have a report we developed that explains all the facts and analysis for every one of these models and styles, and I would be happy to get you a copy of that report if you like.

"But here's what you need to know.

"We found that out of the eight that were left on our list, three of them were just too expensive, which reduced our list to just five.

"And out of those five, we then evaluated which ones were the best value for the money, and only three of them made the cut.

"We only carry those three brands.

"And within those three brands, we carry different models based on different situations that you may have, such as the flooring in your home and the length and style of your carpet.

"We also carry different price ranges because we understand that not everyone can afford a $600 vacuum.

"We get that.

"So, based on what you told me earlier regarding your budget and your flooring situation, you absolutely, positively need this vacuum right here.

"That's the one that will give you everything you need."

This is called power language and when you couple it with a strong opinion, prospects will typically buy from you on the spot.

That's why the next principle on this list is:

Power Talk Principle #5: Tell it like it is.

Don't mince words. If you can't communicate what you do and the benefits you offer in 10 seconds or less, why should you expect any prospect to buy what you sell? Or when a prospect asks you why they should buy from you, you must explain to them your market-dominating position without stuttering or stammering.

They want straight talk. They don't want you to beat around the bush and sugar coat the situation. They want to know the truth. Don't mince words.

Power Talk Principle #6: Use plain English.

Plain English simply means saying it the way people talk. Stop trying to write like Shakespeare and write just like you're speaking to your best friend, because that's the way a prospect likes to be communicated to. You don't "utilize" something, you "use" it. Don't say, *at this point in time.* Say "now." Use plain English.

Power Talk Principle #7: Elevate the attitude.

Speak with passion. Don't just say, (use monotone voice)

> *"Well, we found that there are 52 brands of vacuum cleaners and 44 of them were not up to our standards, so we discarded those, and we looked at the eight that were remaining."*

There's no passion in that. Nobody wants to hear somebody talking about some laboratory tests on some vacuums. Speak with passion and conviction. Here's an assignment for you. Watch TV this next week and watch those legal shows where they're in court and one of the attorneys is defending a client against a lawsuit. I want you to watch the passion of those attorneys. They really get into it. They believe it. They display appropriate passion for the situation. They elevate their attitude in that courtroom and believe me, that attitude affects the jury more often than not.

Power Talk Principle #8: Become your customers' advocate by providing them with genuine advice.

This is how we talk powerfully. Become your customers' advocate in your industry. Tell them the things they need to know and especially what they should know that no one else is telling them. Give them the impression that you're here to help them make the best decision.

Go through that whole scenario I just gave you with the vacuum cleaners a minute ago. Did that sound like I was giving genuine advice, or did it sound like I manufactured that advice? That's because it was passionate. You must be specific. You must tell the story. You must have a strong opinion. You must put it in plain English. You must have passion, elevate the attitude, and all those things add up to becoming your customers' advocate. You're giving them genuine advice. Not, *"Here's what I want you to do because it makes me the most money"* advice, but *genuine* advice. Here's the next thing you need to know.

Power Talk Principle #9: Confidence is not being cocky; it's matter of fact.

Back in the late 90's, announcers would interview Tiger Woods. He stated emphatically that, if he had his game in synch, no one could beat him. Now, was that cocky? No, it was a statement of fact, and everyone watching it from home, everyone on the golf course, including all the other golfers on Tour, all knew it was true. That's *not* cocky; that's confidence!

Power Talk Principle #10: Find and use power words and juicy words.

A juicy word is something that brings out a powerful mental image on the mental canvas of the listener, the hearer, or the viewer. This is something that's hard to teach, but it's easy to look at examples and say - oh, there's a juicy word. And then you can try to insert some juicy words with the power words into your marketing and see if it resonates with your prospects.

Power Talk Principle #11: Concede faults or any downside that there may be.

You may be thinking, "Well, I don't know about telling a prospect that I have certain faults. I don't want to look bad."

Truth be told, if you have some faults, concede them. It gives you credibility when you admit you're not the best in certain situations. There are times when you may not be the best choice.

Think about this. If you draw a line in the sand, then you're going to have to concede the fact that you may not fit certain situations. I'll give you a great example from our vacuum expert. Here's one of the concerns he has.

> *"I'm sure most of you have heard of the Dyson brand vacuum. Dyson has done a wonderful job of marketing their brand, but according to our vacuum expert, it's not a very good vacuum. The reason is because it's bagless. According to our expert, any bagless vacuum is not going to get the job done right, long-term, over time. It's not going to last. It's not going to suck as well as it should, and that's a problem."*

He knows that if he sells a customer a Dyson, it will eventually tarnish his reputation, so he's drawn a line in the sand and refuses to carry that brand. Unfortunately, he said he gets a lot of people walking in asking for the Dyson. When someone requests the Dyson, he tries to convert them to another vacuum. But he admits that some people just want them. They make up approximately 15% of his total vacuum sales. He therefore assumes the role of customer advocate. He tells them that if they want a bagless vacuum, they will have to go somewhere else, because he refuses to sell them since they're a horrible investment. He says something like this,

> *"Look, Dyson's are great looking machines. They're yellow, they look really cool, and the guy in the commercial is European. But I would never let my mother buy one of them. I would never let anyone in my entire family buy one, and I certainly would never let my children buy one. So, I'm not going to let you buy one either."*

Draw that line.

> *"If you don't want to do business with me, that's fine, but I just want you to know that if you buy a Dyson, you're going to buy a mistake."*

See how powerful and convincing this is? This is power talk.

The powerful combination of

- the ignition code
- drawing a line in the sand

- power talk
- social proof
- evidence

will eventually win out, especially when you consider that in almost all cases, the competition is doing nothing like this whatsoever.

These are the 5 key marketing components that will ruin your competition. Use the guidelines covered in this chapter and you will quickly dominate your market.

So now that you know the basic fundamentals involved, in our next chapter I'll show you an actual marketing campaign that was developed for a box manufacturer and how their campaign followed this exact same formula.

This will begin to increase your own marketing knowledge when it comes to effective and compelling marketing and advertising. It will help you to understand why my advertising formula produces real bottom-line results versus the myriad of ads you see and hear in print, on radio and TV, day in and day out.

My job is to provide you with world-class marketing that will separate you from your competition and make you the obvious choice when it comes to buying what you sell.

5 Key Marketing Components That Will Ruin Your Competition
Part 2

This chapter is Part 2 in our lesson on the 5 key marketing components that will ruin your competition. In Part 1, I taught you the 5 components, and showed you how they all work together to produce amazing financial results for any small business owner who understands how to use them.

In this second part of the lesson, I'll show you an actual marketing campaign that was implemented years ago, where the marketing was based solely on the implementation of these 5 marketing components.

Let's begin with a quick review of our previous chapter where we discussed the 5 key marketing components that will ruin your competition. I've mentioned before that marketing depends on your ability to establish trust, respect, and rapport. You won't establish any of these if you can't convey the fact that you're credible.

The 5 key marketing components that will ruin your competition are also the 5 components that will establish your credibility with your prospects.

The 5 components are:

1. The Ignition Code,
2. Drawing a line in the sand,
3. Using powerful language,
4. Social proof, and
5. Evidence.

We're going to spend most of the time talking about #2 and #3—drawing a line in the sand and using powerful language. But let me remind you again what the "ignition code" is referring to, and the critical importance it plays in the overall success of *any* business.

The "ignition code" comes from a movie called "The Transporter." It means that no matter what you do, whatever your business, your competition can't touch you. You simply offer more value than anyone else in your industry. A prospect would be an absolute fool if they bought what you sell from anyone else but you, period! That's an ignition code. In short, it refers to your market-dominating position. When you have an ignition code, you automatically become more confident. And confidence is what customers and prospects are looking for from the businesses they transact with.

So, in this chapter, we're going to combine *drawing a line in the sand*, along with *power talk*, and add a touch of *the Ignition Code* attitude to show you how all three of these components worked together to create a market dominating advertising campaign for a small but aggressive box manufacturer.

The company I want to use as our example is called Bana Box. This is a company that sells boxes, the kind that manufacturers use to ship their products to various customers and retail stores. For instance, one of their customers is Nokia. Bana Box doesn't produce the box that a Nokia phone goes into, but they do produce the box that 20 or 30 phones go into so they can ship their phones over to various retailers.

These are referred to as shipping containers and they're different from what you might call "retail" boxes. Bana Box has built their core business around operations and production.

They have systems in place for getting orders done fast, and they've offered emergency rush service for their best customers in the past. The ads I'm going to show you here actually go back to the late 90s. I realize this is a little dated, but I did this intentionally to show you that solid marketing fundamentals always stand the test of time. These ads will illustrate the principles we've just discussed perfectly. Remember, this chapter isn't about marketing examples; it's about teaching you how to create your own ignition code, how to draw a line in the sand, and how to use powerful language. We'll also touch briefly on ways to use social proof and how to present evidence.

Bana Box was in the process of building a new factory so they could increase their capacity to ship both regular and rush orders, and the owner said that he could provide rush shipments for all his customers and prospects, without creating any additional bottlenecks in production. Think about that for a minute.

No other box company in the world could do that at the time. That gives them their own "ignition code."

Now is the time for them to draw a line in the sand. They're the company that does boxes fast. And if that's the line they've drawn, everything they do must now reflect that position.

For example, they created a logo to reflect their new position. That logo needs to convey the fact that they provide boxes fast.

Does this logo fit that description? Answer, yes.

Then they put together a logo that says, "custom boxes on your dock in just four hours, guaranteed."

This was a secondary logo to talk about a guarantee that they put into place to go with their fast box position. Now, watch how this begins to roll out as we start to convey this

message in their marketing, starting with the headlines in their ads.

Now remember, this is called Power Talk. We're going to start with some headlines, and then I'll show you some marketing pieces that were used to dramatically increase this company's revenue. Here's the first headline they used:

"When DFW's biggest companies need boxes NOW, here's who they call."

The keyword used in this ad is "now".

Headline number two:

"Whoever heard of ordering a custom box and having it ready on your dock in just four hours."

Headline number three:

"Whose fault is it when you run out of boxes and your line shuts down? I say it's your box supplier's fault."

See how this uses power language? I want you to keep in mind the principles we've discussed so far—being specific, telling the story, have a strong opinion, and so on. Watch how all these principles start to show up in these headlines. Notice how they all draw that line in the sand! Next headline:

"Have you ever been shellacked by your boss for running out of boxes and your line shutting down?"

There's a great power word, a great juicy word—*shellacked*! Next headline:

"Revolutionary new box making system developed. Any box custom made from scratch and delivered to your dock within four hours, guaranteed."

Here are a few more headlines:

"To purchasing agents who never ever want to run out of boxes again, even once."

Again, we've got power words here. Never. Ever. Not even once. See how clear this is, how specific it is? See the line being drawn in the sand?

"How to have custom boxes delivered to your dock in just four hours or less, even from scratch."

"How a company that designs, makes, and delivers custom boxes in less than four hours saved my job."

This is called "telling a story."

"Purchasing managers who have never run out of boxes and had to shut down production are not invited to read this card."

This is Power Talk. You don't talk like this if you're timid or meek. You talk like that when you're powerful, when you're confident, when you have an ignition code.

"Custom boxes on your dock in 4 hours, or they're free."

That's just an articulation of their logo.

"Suppose you unexpectedly ran out of boxes and caused your production line to shut down for three days."

"If your box supplier is late, you could get fired. Take this precautionary move and rest assured you will never run out of boxes again."

Wow, fired.

"Run out of boxes and have to shut down your production lines. Here are four excuses that will work with your boss and three that won't."

"Speed and reliability. Two things your current supplier hopes and prays you will never ask him to do."

This is powerful language, it's "power talk". Look at this last one again. It doesn't matter what those two things are. Now, obviously it matters to this company in the context of this ad. But from a discussion standpoint, it doesn't matter what those two things are.

Here's what I mean. Can any company really say something like "two things your supplier hopes and prays you will never ask him to do" unless you've got something powerful to say? No. See, this is called "power talk." People look at that and say, "Wow, these guys must be serious." And the answer is, yeah, they are serious. Here's an interesting headline,

"How to cram a box supplier order that normally takes six days to fill down to just four hours. It only takes one phone call."

See the power word in there? Cram.

Here's a letter that was sent out to prospects, and I'll highlight one specific part here.

"I Can Personally Guarantee That You Will Never Run Out Of Shipping Boxes Again, Even In Your Most Critical, Time-Sensitive Situations."

"Dear Jim: If you've ever been in a box emergency where you've had to shut down your production lines because you were out of boxes, then this letter might be of particular interest to you."

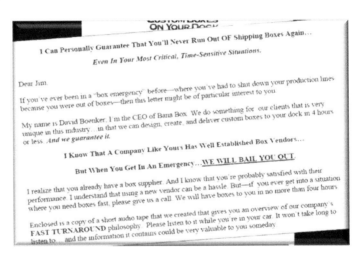

We open with this statement because most of the people that get this letter have had that scenario happen to them.

"My name is David Banker. I'm the CEO of Bana Box. We do something for our clients that is very unique in this industry, in that we can design, create and deliver custom boxes to your dock in four hours or less, and we guarantee it."

Now, let me highlight several points that we just made here. Number 1: *No one else can do this.* That was this company's ignition code, right? Number 2: *Four hours or less.* Then bold and italicized "***And we guarantee it***". This is called elevating the attitude in print. And we can guarantee it. I want you to understand how powerful that is when it's read by the prospects.

"I know that a company like yours has well-established box vendors, but when you get in an emergency, we will bail you out."

Look at that juicy phrase. We will bail you out. This is nothing short of brilliant in terms of getting people to understand that you've got something powerful.

"I realize that you already have a box supplier. And I know that you're probably satisfied with their performance. I understand that using a new vendor can be a hassle. But - if you ever get into a situation where you need boxes fast, please give us a call. We will have boxes to you in no more than four hours."

Now, let's look at some of the pieces that were put together to send out to this company's prospects. I want you to look at the fonts. Bear in mind that these were actually designed to be faxed out back in the late 90's when faxing was more of an accepted practice. That rarely happens these days. But that doesn't mean we couldn't still use these

today. They would easily convert to direct mail or email campaigns. Let's look at this.

"Purchasing managers who have never run out of boxes - and had to shut down production - are not invited to read this message."

Again, understand that most prospects receiving this communication have had that exact situation happen to them. *"Even if you think you will never need boxes in four hours, keep this paper. Someday you'll be glad you have it. At Bana, we don't just talk about great customer service. Our trucks deliver your boxes to your dock in four hours or less to prove it."* This is called Power Talk. Think about this for a minute, who talks like this? Answer, a company that has drawn a line in the sand talks like this.

Go back to that list we covered in Part 1.

- Be specific.
- Acknowledge concerns. You don't think you're going to even need this, so I acknowledge that concern.
- Tell the Story.
- Have a Strong Opinion.
- Tell it like it is. Don't mince words.
- Use plain English.
- Elevate the attitude. Say it with passion.
- Be the customer's advocate. Give genuine advice.
- Be matter of fact, not cocky.
- Use Power words and Juicy words.
- Concede your faults or downside.

Keep revisiting these to make sure you incorporate them into your marketing when appropriate.

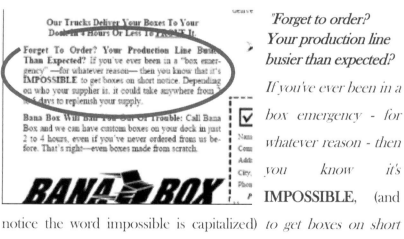

"Forget to order? Your production line busier than expected?

If you've ever been in a box emergency - for whatever reason - then you know it's IMPOSSIBLE, (and notice the word impossible is capitalized) *to get boxes on short notice. Depending on who your supplier is, it could take anywhere from two to five days to replenish your supply.* **Bana Box will bail you out of trouble.** *Call Bana Box and we can have custom boxes on* *your dock in just two to four hours, even if you've never ordered from us before. That's right - even boxes made from scratch. Join companies like Nokia and Seicor who wouldn't risk their orders with anyone else."* By highlighting Nokia and Seicor here, we start to get into the use of social proof.

Next example:

"Suppose you unexpectedly ran out of boxes and had to shut down your production line for three days. Do you have a backup plan? Next time you need custom boxes NOW, and your current supplier can't get it in time, let us design, produce and deliver your order in just four hours. You don't have to switch suppliers," (gain, we're acknowledging their concern here), **"just let us pinch hit when you need it most. We know you've got a good supplier. We know you won't just up and switch, so we're not asking you to switch. But if you get caught in the troublesome position of needing boxes fast, and your normal supplier can't get the job done, Bana Box will bail you out of trouble."**

Let me explain what's happening here. This is taking advantage of the concept known as *accelerated discontentment.* We know that the hot

92

buttons we're targeting here are the problems that frequently occur in this industry. Every time we convey the fact that we can deliver boxes to their dock in 4 hours or less, it cements their discontentment with their current box supplier. They begin to question why their current supplier can't fulfill on this same promise.

Now, the more we continue to contact them and drive this point home, the greater their discontentment grows, until one day they *will* hit the breaking point. This fax campaign I'm showing you was designed to be a multi-touch campaign where prospects were hit again and again and again and again. So, think about that for a minute. Here's what's going to happen.

They're going to look at this, and say,

"Gosh, have I ever been in this situation, and if I was, what did my supplier do? Oh yeah, they let me down because they couldn't get my boxes to me. Here's a company that can fix that and they're talking with powerful language. They're not saying they may be able to do this. They're saying they will do this. They're saying they will guarantee they will do this."

So always remember the concept of accelerated discontentment, and watch how we keep pounding this concept into their heads with this next ad.

This specific campaign for Bana Box had an additional 20 or so of these types of ads. And they all continued to emphasize this company's ignition code. They drew the line in the sand, they used power talk, they contained social proof, and they presented evidence that was compelling and that built credibility. This fax campaign was designed to reach its targeted prospects once every two weeks for an entire year. Of course, the big question is this, was it effective? Did it produce measurable results?

Bana Box went from a $3 million per year company to a $70 million per year company on the back of this fax campaign.

The powerful combination of

1. The Ignition Code,
2. Drawing a line in the sand,
3. Using powerful language,
4. Social proof, and
5. Evidence

will eventually win out, especially when you consider that in almost all cases, the competition is doing nothing like this whatsoever.

How To Write Copy Better Than the Pros

This chapter is going to show you how to write copy better than professional copywriters. For your marketing and advertising to generate more leads and attract more clients, you must learn how to structure your marketing message so that's it's both irresistible and compelling. When you acquire the ability to write in a compelling way, you can turn your business into what we call a "profit faucet".

This simply means that when you need more business, your superior and persuasive marketing can be turned on like the faucet in your kitchen, generating all the leads your business can handle. When you start to reach your maximum capacity, you can turn your marketing off until you need it again. Imagine having that type of control over your business. That's how you begin to finally achieve financial freedom.

To create a truly compelling message, you must learn to create "persuasion marketing". We've created a template to help you do this better than the pros. In fact, with just a little practice following our template, you will be able to write sales copy and scripts better than 95% of all copywriters available today.

We call it our Compelling Message Template and it's designed to provide you with a paint-by-numbers outline for writing any type of compelling marketing messaging, including powerful sales or video scripts, sales letters, cold-call letters, voice mail messages, or face-to-face sales scripts. That's quite a template, isn't it? Master it, and it will make you a fortune.

One thing though before we continue. You might become confused as to how this template differs from an elevator pitch template. At first glance, they may appear to be very close in design. That's because they *are* and it's critical to your success as a small business owner to understand why.

Our marketing is based on a tested and proven formula we call the Conversion Equation... **Interrupt, Engage, Educate** and **Offer**. Those four components *must* be used in all your sales and marketing collateral going forward. That's because the Conversion Equation follows the exact same formula as the human mind uses to make important decisions. So naturally every template we use will follow that exact same format.

Let's then look at our "wealth-creating" Compelling Message Template and explain the eight-step format that works so well.

 Step #1: Begin with an *attention-grabbing, interrupting* headline or opening paragraph focused on a problem, fear, frustration, or concern. This means to always begin each type of communication with an all-important "grabber." This may be the headline in a letter or email or, if that isn't appropriate for your business, then the grabber should be the first sentence or the first paragraph.

If you're using radio, the grabber must be the first thing your listeners hear. If you use local broadcast or cable TV, it must be the first thing your viewers see and hear.

It's vital that you always begin every marketing piece you create with an attention-grabbing, hot button-hitting opening that *figuratively* smacks your prospects across the face and all but forces them to pay attention to your message.

It's like driving past a terrible car accident. You don't want to look but you simply can't resist a glance. It's just too compelling.

That's why you must start every message with an attention-grabbing, interrupting headline or opening statement. If you don't, no one will bother to read the rest of your message, no matter how well you write it.

Step #2: *Engage* your prospects by promising them a solution to the problem in the opener. Remember that your prospects don't care anything about you. They don't care what you have named your business, or what you look like, or that you've been in business for thirty-five years. They don't care about any of that. They only care about finding the solution to the problem they have. It really is that simple.

This is where you very briefly explain your product or service, and its benefits and features. Focus heavily on the *benefits* because ultimately, that's what prospects buy. Never forget the old saying, "features tell, benefits sell". After you interrupt them with your opening statement or paragraph, *engage* them by explaining how they will *benefit* if they keep reading or listening to your message.

Are you starting to get the hang of this? The headline must describe the problem in your prospect's life, and the sub-headline promises them that there's a solution to that problem.

It doesn't *give* them the solution; it just *promises* there is a solution. They will need to continue through the rest of the message if they want to discover the actual solution. It's the *promise* of the solution that engages the prospect and keeps them engaged in reading or listening to your message.

See how this template makes this a paint-by-numbers exercise?

Step #3: State the reason they should purchase the product or service. Remember that all prospects make *two* buying decisions when they purchase anything. They first decide to buy the product or service, and then they decide *who* they will buy it from.

This explains why so many businesses compete on price. I first decide I'll buy a new car by selecting the make and model I want, and then I go to only those dealerships that sell that make and model and choose the dealer that gives me the "best deal." The key words here are *best deal, not lowest price.*

The single biggest mistake all small business owners make today is they blindly assume all their prospects are only shopping for the lowest price. And in most cases, they're absolutely right. Their prospects are indeed shopping for the lowest price, simply because the business owner hasn't given them any other value proposition that proves their business is any different from their competitors.

Your prospects are *not* shopping for the lowest price. They *are* shopping for the best deal. That means they're looking for the most *value* for the price they do pay.

Your job as a small business owner is to innovate your business so you offer more value than your competition does. You must find a way to offer a much higher value proposition than anyone else in your industry. We often refer to this as creating your market dominating position. What is it that makes your business unique? What is it that differentiates and separates your business from your competition? What do your customers buy from you, and you alone. That's your market dominating position.

So first, always look for ways to create additional value for your prospects and highlight that value in step three when using the Compelling Message Template. That establishes the reason why they should buy the product or service from you, and you alone.

Step #4: Tell them what you will do to help them gain the benefits. Tell them exactly what you will do to assist them with their purchase decision.

Perhaps you will give them a complementary bottle of champagne for ordering at your restaurant or staying at your hotel, or you might provide them with a free home cleaning after they purchase their first one. Never keep them guessing. Let them know right up front what you do to ensure they receive the benefits you promise and the features you will provide.

 Step #5: Be specific about the actions *they* will take. If you don't tell your prospects what to do, they won't do it, plain and simple. If you want them to download your free report, then you must instruct them to do so, and make it very obvious how they should go about doing just that.

 Step #6: Offer them a bonus or some form of compelling incentive when practical. Everyone loves to feel like they're getting a "deal". So, if it's appropriate, go ahead and sweeten the pot.

For example, if you own an oil change shop and you send your prospects an offer to change their oil at their next appointment for $19.95, then offer them a bonus discount if they agree to let you change their transmission oil at the same appointment. Instead of them paying the normal price of $79.95, you will discount that service to $59.95.

If you sell men's suits, offer them a bonus such as a free silk tie with every suit they purchase or 50% off all dress shirts.

Remember what we said earlier about value. Prospects buy value, not price. So whenever appropriate, offer an incentive or bonus that continues to add additional value to what you sell.

 Step #7: Reverse their potential risk using powerful guarantees. When a prospect contemplates making a purchase, they mentally go through a risk – reward analysis. They compare the benefits they think they'll receive with the potential risks they may incur if the product or service fails to deliver as advertised.

I see most small business owners today offering 100% money back guarantees. They think that it is the ultimate risk reversal technique and, by offering it, they create an irresistible offer.

They're somewhat misguided though. Please don't misunderstand me. If you sell a high dollar product or service, then guaranteeing the prospect that they will receive 100% of their money back is indeed a powerful risk reversal technique. But most small business owners don't sell high ticket items.

If you sell something for under $100, the hassle and wasted time that's involved in getting a refund is often more of an issue to the typical prospect than the return of their money.

That's why a 100% money back guarantee has all but lost its appeal in today's time-starved society. The process required to get our money back just isn't worth the time and hassle involved to do it unless it's a big-ticket item.

My point here is to find a way to completely remove all risk to your prospects and do it in such a way that they view it as truly 100% risk free to them in every sense of the word. Let them know that not only is their money not at risk, but neither is their time, effort, and energy.

Look at your own business and ask yourself how you can come up with something similar. If something goes wrong with what you sell, how can you eliminate any hassle on the part of your prospects? Can you go to their home to perform a repair, or take them a replacement product?

If you provide a service, can you offer a 14-day satisfaction guarantee where if they're not satisfied, they have 14 days to contact you and you'll come back and perform the service until they are satisfied? And if you don't know what would totally remove the risk for your prospects when they buy what you sell, then just ask them. Believe me, they'll be happy to tell you.

And **Step #8:** Always end with a **P.S.** and use it to restate the benefits. This is important if your message is in writing. However, if your message is being delivered verbally, then simply summarize your key benefits at the end of your message. There's an old saying, "last thing heard, first thing remembered". The last things you always want your prospects to see or hear are the key benefits you will provide to them. Restate the most compelling part of your message and drive it home to your prospects.

Follow these eight steps when delivering any type of message, and that message will compel your prospects to take immediate action.

You now have a paint-by-numbers template to guide you each and every time you need to create any type of sales message. And you'll do so with more confidence and certainty. And maybe, best of all, this will position you light years ahead of your competition.

Grow Your Business Fast Through a Publicity and PR Campaign

I'm going to be up front with you. Growing your business through a systematic publicity or public relations campaign is powerful but ... it is a *field* of study. Books have been written on it. Multi-day seminars have been given around it. People make careers out of it. So please look at this chapter as one that sparks your imagination and, hopefully, a springboard to further study.

It is impossible to overestimate the value of Publicity and PR. A business could spend $5,000 or more on a newspaper advertisement and not see any increase in business. But if there is an aspect of your business that the public might find fascinating (or if you can create one), you can get on TV, radio, and in the newspaper as a feature story. The value of that story is worth possibly *five times* the value of an ad that takes up similar time or space. Here's the reason:

When you place an ad in the media, the public knows that you are promoting yourself and they tend to be skeptical. When the media takes the time or space to run a story on you, then it gives credibility to you. The public thinks (subconsciously, at least), "If the media is interviewing her, she must be legitimate."

An English Conversation School owner in Japan understood the power of media. He owned a chain of schools but faced fierce competition from national chains.

To combat them, he wrote a short book which he called, Ultimate Study Secrets", self-published it, then secured the endorsement of the former Japanese Minister of Education. He then went to the local Board of Education office and asked if he could give a copy to every student graduating from Elementary School in the city. They agreed if he didn't give away any literature that promoted his school. He was thrilled with that condition.

In two months, he got to put a book in the hand of every 6th-grade student in the city. When it came time to give books to the students where his own children went to school, he had his secretary call all the media outlets in the surrounding area. Three newspapers and the TV station showed up and the story was carried in every media outlet. Then the local radio station called to interview him. He went into the studio and gave a 30-minute interview. They replayed that interview *every day* for a week.

Every student going into the pressure years of Junior High School got to meet him. More importantly, the mothers became aware of him; they were the decision makers.

His wife took the idea of free publicity a step further. She met with a Japanese friend, and they came up with an idea for a TV show which they called *English Studio.* She was on TV nearly every week for two years! It's no wonder their competitors quit the game completely, closed shop, and left. They had a corner on the market.

Your business might not have the same advantage. However, you can

105

find something that the media finds worthy of attention.

Consider for just a moment the example of an Australian business that runs a special event promotion every working day of the year! It is such a phenomenon that they publish a calendar of special events that draws them attention all over their city. Examples of their special promotions include "Best-salad-made-in-the-store-wins-two-free-movie-passes-Day".

There are no limitations to the number of special events you can run, except the limitations that you place upon your creativity and imagination. Why not 50, or 100 or 300? Start dreaming up what you can do, make them appropriate for your business and watch what happens. If no one else in your industry is doing special events, it gives you a very clear edge.

With each special event, you can get media coverage. Think of it this way:

In most towns and cities, there are talk radio stations. There's normally a morning talk show that runs from 7 am to 11 am, Monday to Friday. That's 4 hours a day, 5 days a week, 50 weeks of the year. That's 1,000 hours of talk radio that they must fill every year. There's one thing the talk show hosts *must* have—an abundance of interesting stories! That's where you come in.

They *don't* want you to call them and tell them about your product or service with the idea that they're going to act as your salesperson.

No! They want a story! If you're ever listened to the radio or watched TV, the host of the show will leave people with a hook right before going to a commercial break. They want people to stick around so they must put out a hook.

"Right after the break, we're going to talk to someone who can show you how to lose weight without exercise or eating less."

That would be a good hook for someone in the diet industry who shows people how to raise their metabolism through breathing exercises.

When you have decided on your hook, it's time to write a press release. You can put out a press release through a company like PRWeb (www.PRWeb.com) that have an abundance of resources from strategy, to "How to Write a Press Release", and much more. The pricing is very reasonable, and it *could* be effective. One interview could change everything for you.

Once you have appeared in a media interview, you can request a copy of that interview and leverage that to get even more media. If you can state on your website, "As Seen on Fox & Friends", then it increases your credibility. Remember, the higher the trust, the greater the sales.

The very best way to be interviewed in the media is to go in person to the media office and hand your press release to the secretary, with a short note for the name of the host of the show or the producer.

If you are selected for an interview, send the host of the show a list of "suggested questions" and then bring that list with you as well. Remember that talk show hosts are busy. When you give them a list of questions, they will thank you because you've done a lot of their job for them, and it saves them going out and researching more about who you are and then what questions they should ask. Realize, however, that they might not stick to your questions as you wrote them and are, in fact, likely to diverge a fair amount. However, it will give you the opportunity to prepare adequately for the interview and shape its overall direction.

Making it Practical

There are three main components of an effective Publicity strategy.

1) Identify something (or many things) noteworthy about your business that the public might find amusing, amazing, or newsworthy.
2) Prepare for the media
   A) Create a Press Release
   B) Build a media page on your site
      a) About you
      b) Hooks
      c) Suggested questions
      d) Testimonials
      e) Images

C) Prepare for the interviews

    a) Role play and practice

2) Contact the media

    A) Telephone

    B) Press release

Who is responsible for publicity and public relations in your company?

Recognizing that free publicity has at least 5x the impact of an ad, what impact do you think it would have on your business if you could increase the occurrence of free publicity?

If you don't have someone responsible for publicity and PR in your business, why not bring in someone who can help you?

Direct Mail
The Army of Salespeople

With all the hype on social media marketing, many business owners have turned their back on traditional marketing campaigns such as direct mail.

This presents an opportunity for you. New technologies like GeoFarming can help marketers know exactly who to send direct mail pieces to.

What is GeoFarming? GeoFarming allows a marketer to select an area of their neighborhood or city and find out the details of who lives in each house. So instead of blanketing an area of the city "hoping" some of your ideal customers live in a percent of the houses, marketers can now pre-select the homes that their ideal clients live in. This allows a direct mail campaign to be tremendously more profitable.

Using direct mail is like having an army of salespeople in the field. The advantage is that they get into the homes or businesses at a very low cost and have the chance to tell the full story in a carefully crafted proposition. The disadvantage could be that they are discarded without being opened, or they are deleted if they are emails.

This chapter takes you through the beginning steps of what it takes to use direct mail as a marketing arm of your business. You must begin to understand the components of a superior direct mail package and letter. This is, by far, easier said than done. Expecting me to explain this to you in one short chapter is comparable to asking a doctor to explain the elements of surgery in five minutes—sure you'll get the basics, but it must be for a springboard for your own further study.

You have four primary goals. Your job is to ensure that your direct mail piece is:

1) Delivered,
2) Opened,
3) Read,
4) Responded to with the action you desire.

To do this, we're going to first look at the components of a great direct mail package and letter.

Here are the **5 Components of a Great Mail Package**:

1. The envelope. It must be enticing enough that a person wants to open it, and it must not be confused with junk mail, or it's sure to be thrown straight into the trash. The job of the envelope is to get the recipient to open it. You can put an enticing headline on the envelope, or you may leave it plain and blank (except for the address, of course). You won't know what works best for your offer until you test both approaches.

2. The letter. This is your sales pitch in writing. Remember this: if you cannot sell in person, you will never sell in print. It must be well-written, and it can be compared to a greased slide – someone starts at the top and slides all the way down without so much as catching themselves on any nail that sticks up.

Here are the **8 Elements of a Super Sales Letter:**

a) A headline that compels the reader to read on,
b) A compelling offer that creates a desire or need for your product or service,
c) Strong reasons why your product or service will fill that need or satisfy that desire—the benefits of your product or service, not just the features,
d) Testimonials showing how other people have benefited from your product or service,
e) The answers to all major questions that people might ask,
f) A risk-reversal or guarantee so that people feel secure in their ordering,
g) A strong close where you compel people to act now,
h) A P.S. showing another great benefit and call to action—this is the second most read part of the letter.

3. **The brochure.** These can be inserted with the letter, and it furthers your sales pitch.

4. **The order form.** Make sure it is very easy to understand. Remember the K.I.S.S. formula—Keep It Simple Stupid! No offense intended, but just remember not to get too fancy here. An alternative to an order form is a coupon that can be inserted into the body of the letter. Remember to make it stand out—use a different color so it can't be missed.

5. **The reply envelope (optional).** You must make it easy for a customer to return his order form to you. Alternately, you want to have a phone number where people can call you, OR a website that they can easily type into their browser. However, it should not be your main landing page—you must know clearly which visitors are coming from your direct mail campaign.

Millions of letters have been tested over time through the major publishing houses. Usually, if you don't include a reply envelope, simply give just one phone number to call. This will give you the highest response.

Direct mail can also be viewed as a revenue generator, not an expense. Everything in marketing is a test ... until it proves to be successful. If you think that direct mail might hold promise for you or your client, you can test small.

- Send 500 letters to a sample of your target audience. (The cost could be anywhere from $500 to $1,000.)
- See what response you get. If you bring in orders where the profits of these orders exceed the cost of the campaign, then you have a successful campaign which can even be improved through split testing. If the response is less than optimal, you still might be able to make it profitable through split testing. For small businesses, the risk is low given the relatively low expense.

Let's now discuss split testing. With direct mail, you can precisely test the percent of return you get, and you'll know exactly whether to continue or discontinue. Let's say that you want to send 10,000 letters to homes in your city. It would be a mistake to create one letter and send it to all 10,000 homes when you could split test a basic element of your direct mail package and gain an advantage. *One* way to do this would be to send 1,000 letters with one type of envelope and another 1,000 letters with a different type of envelope. You wait and see which envelope creates the greatest response and then send the remaining 8,000 letters using the winning formula.

Let's see how the impact on this split test from a financial viewpoint and we'll keep our numbers round and simple for easy math.

Perhaps you sell a product and service combination that brings you customers with a lifetime value of $1,000. Your standard letter pulls a 1% response (for example). Out of 10,000 letters you send, you get 100 orders at $1,000 each for a total of $100,000 revenue.

If you *first* split test the envelope only and your standard letter got a 1% response, but your second letter got a 1.1% response, then the result would look like this:

1,000 letters x 1% response = 10 sales x $1,000 = $10,000

1,000 letters x 1.1% response = 11 sales x $1,000 = $11,000

(Then send out the remaining 8,000 letters using the winning envelope.)

8,000 letters x 1.1% response = 88 sales x $1,000 = $88,000

Total Sales: $109,000

The increase is $9,000 or 9% simply because you took the time to test. As a micro-business, you can even test as few as 100 letters at a time and still find improvements that you could build upon.

What kinds of elements can you test? You can test:

- The envelope design
- The type of paper you use

- The length of the letter
- The font (type and colors)
- The headline (and sub-headline)
- The compelling offer
- The call to action
- Images
- The body text (layout, length of paragraphs, etc.)
- Testimonials
- Guarantee or how you reverse their risk
- Whether or not to include a return envelope
- Envelope stuffers (inclusion of promotional items that you might tie into the body of your letter)

You could boost the effectiveness of the campaign if you followed up on the mailing with a phone call. A simple opening script could be: "Mr. Jones, I sent you a letter earlier this week. I just wanted to make sure you got the letter, and you understand the offer."

This is worth testing if you have the manpower or ability to do it. A follow-up call might boost the response by 5% or 10%. Do your calculations and see if it makes sense to add this element to your campaign.

How To Send Direct Mail To 50,000 Qualified Prospects For FREE!

Besides having a compelling offer, the key to successful marketing is repetition. The more times that you can put a compelling offer in front of your ideal prospects, the more likely it is that they'll take the step and investigate what it is you are offering.

Because of the proliferation in marketing today, experts now say it takes between seven to twenty-one individual contacts or touch points to establish sufficient trust, respect, and rapport to get a prospect to buy what you sell.

So how can financially strapped small business owners accomplish this seemingly impossible task? Most of them attempt email solicitations. That's normally a complete waste of time. Just look at your own response to emails. You probably delete them without even opening them. The only exception to this rule is using joint venture partnerships, and only then if your JV partner has an excellent relationship with their database prospects. Most of them don't.

If you're willing to devote a little time and effort to this direct mail marketing strategy, the cost for you to reach multiple prospects multiple times will be negligible. Just follow these steps to send direct mail to 50,000 qualified prospects for free!

#1: Discover your ideal client. This is the client that wants what you sell versus *needs* what you sell. I *need* to have my dentist fill a cavity... but I certainly don't *want* it. On the other hand, no one *needs* whiter teeth... but most of us *want* whiter teeth.

Can you see the difference in these two situations? Wants are based on emotion and needs are based on logic. Discovering your ideal client depends on your ability to discover their physical demographic traits as well as their emotional psychographic traits.

#2: Map out their decision-making process. All human beings want the best deal. That doesn't mean lowest price, but it does mean the most *value* for the price. Prospects will pay twice the price of your competitors if they see five times the value for the price you charge them. Prospects decide to buy based on value, so map out what your ideal clients consider valuable to them in their specific situation.

A daycare mother with a 6-month-old infant will value a daycare that offers sufficient staff trained to show additional love, care, and support for the kids they keep. On the other hand, a daycare mom with a 4-year-old child will value a daycare that specializes in offering educational program for preschoolers. Wouldn't any daycare mom want her child to be reading at a first-grade level prior to kindergarten?

#3: Create a compelling message, once the innovations are in place. This should be easy to do since the innovations typically separate the business from all competitors. Writing a compelling message becomes as simple as stating the facts... listing the differences between you and your competition.

Now use this strategy to get your message out to your ideal clients.

1. Create a list of additional products and services that your ideal clients favor. If you're a landscaper, your ideal clients would be interested in adding a fence to their yard, or perhaps a pool, stonework, a barbeque pit, or a patio deck. They may want their home painted, their bathroom remodeled, their home inspected, a security system installed, and so on.

None of these are direct competitors with the landscaper, but they *all* should be targeting the same "ideal" client.

2. Pick up the phone and call as many of each of these businesses as required until you find one of them... and only one... from each type of business that would be willing to partner with you on a direct mail marketing program. You should plan to find a minimum of 10 non-competitive businesses to partner with.

3. Each partner is responsible for designing a 3 x 5 or a 4 x 6 "minimum-sized" postcard with a special offer listed on it for their business... similar to what you often see in a "Valpak" mailing. You will agree to coordinate buying the prospect list from the list broker that fits your ideal client description, arrange the printing of all the postcards, getting the postcards to the direct mail house and

scheduling the various mailings over whatever time frame the group decides is appropriate.

In short, you're going to create your very own Valpak business consortium, with you at the helm. Before you contact any potential partners, check out the costs for all these services and arrange for bulk discounting with the printer and mail house. Know what your costs are for everything. Be sure to look online as there are a multitude of reputable online printers and mass mailers offering bulk pricing.

Typically, you can send out direct mail postcards for around seventy cents each... but that's when you send them individually. You're going to send ALL your partner's postcards... as well as your own in a single mailing.

So, if you target 10,000 homes in your area that are your ideal clients, the total cost to mail those prospects one time may be around $5000 to $6000, including purchasing a multiple use mailing list. Naturally prices will vary depending on your location, etc.

By the way, that price should also include the printing and mailing of *your* postcard as well... and your postcard is *not* going to be a "minimum-sized" 3 x 5 or a 4 x 6. *Yours* will be a 6 x 11 full color postcard so it stands out from all the others.

Please note that your partners may also create this same sized postcard, but by stating they are to provide you with a "minimum-sized" 3 x 5 or 4 x 6 card, they will automatically request that size for their mailing. They can always upgrade in the future if they so desire. Most won't, and yours will stand out from the others when prospects open the mailer.

4. Gain all the partners agreement that you will schedule a minimum of 10 separate mailings for a total cost of $50,000... which is $5000 per mailing times 10 mailings. That's only $5000 per business owner, and they can pay that on a per mailing basis. Ten separate mailings may take 5 months to complete, so that's a $1000 per month marketing budget.

Realistically, out of 10,000 recipients, every business in this consortium could easily expect to gain a minimum of 10 new clients. That's 1/10 of 1% *only*. This is an *extremely* conservative figure. Many of these direct mail campaigns average one half of one percent, which would mean an average of 50 new clients. And that's after a single mailing... this is a total of ten mailings. *Wow*!

By the way, look at *your* investment in all of this. All you have invested in this entire process is your time and organizational skills and your oversized postcard should pull two to three times more clients than your partners, your partners have covered all costs involved, and you have certainly earned your free ride by coordinating this entire process and driving qualified clients to them in droves. This is a true win-win scenario, especially for business owners with zero marketing dollars.

In fact, there are several companies that will provide this service for you. They're called "card deck" mailings. But you can save a lot of money doing these mailings yourself. They're very easy to do. And I believe in the saying that "if you want it done right, do it yourself." It's always best to control the process yourself.

But whether you do it yourself or use a company that specializes in card deck mailings, this is a very cost-effective way to advertise a business if you're trading area is local.

Here's the thing: You can now actually make money in two businesses.

You will make money on the business you're promoting in your mailing -- that is, with your own postcard. And you can make a lot of money selling postcards to your co-op mailing partners. Just mark up the cost 15% or so -- not so big a mark-up that your co-op partners resent your profit. A 15% mark-up to compensate you for your work and initiative is certainly reasonable, and you'll still be underpricing the big national "card deck" mailing services.

You can start mailing these co-op mailings once a month, and then maybe move to once a week. I think you can see how you can make some great money at this. If you've got some ambition, working this system up to a point where you're mailing 100,000 card decks and other co-op mailings per week is no big leap.

And don't get the impression that this is a "get-rich-quick" project. Getting this system up and running will take time, effort, and energy on your part. But for if you are a small business owner with little to no marketing dollars, this is a strategy that's definitely worth investigating.

At a minimum, use this little trick to conduct direct mail marketing campaigns for no cost to you. It's not too hard to find 10 to 12 businesses that will be more than happy to jump in and do a joint venture with you.

I hope this chapter has provided you with the step-by-step tactical approaches you need to properly execute this dynamic direct mail strategy. Lead generation drives revenue for all small businesses. Now you know the steps to a great direct mail campaign, and you have the additional ability to send direct mail to 50,000 qualified prospects for free!

The Power of Scripts to "Exponentialize" Your Growth

It is often quoted in business circles that the quality of your life and business is determined by the quality of your communication. Whether you memorize scripts or not, it must be understood that *everyone* uses scripts – that is to say, everyone communicates with specific words that they have consciously or subconsciously prepared. It makes sense that if one could prepare their communication with a definite purpose (like preparing for a speech), that the quality of that communication will be at a higher level.

Preparing scripts allows you to prepare for your communication with potential clients so that your words are strategic and impacting, thus resulting in more sales.

Every business owner should have a variety of scripts at their disposal. These may include the following:

1. Initial presentation/opening scripts

These are like the headlines in an advertisement. People will size you up in seconds and if aren't razor-sharp from the very first word, you may well lose the sale.

I recently walked into a store and the owner asked, "How are y'all doing today?" I said, "Fine" as I found my way past him ... out the door. What if he had riveted me to the spot with an intriguing question? For example, "Did you happen to see our amazing coupon in this week's paper?" Wouldn't that get your attention?

2. Question scripts

When you ask great questions, it validates you as the authority. Do you have a memorized series of questions that you ask prospective clients? Perhaps you can ask questions that cause them to think, "Incredible! I need to talk to him/her more!" I love to ask questions to prospects or clients that they know they *should* be asking. That's one of the reasons I use the Profit Acceleration Software™. It helps me ask brilliant questions that people know they should be asking but aren't.

3. Scripts for dealing with concerns, frustrations, and objections

You will face concerns, frustrations, and objections from your prospects and clients. Just like the FAQ (Frequently Asked Questions), there are Frequently Stated Concerns, Frustrations, and Objections. You (or your staff) will know what the primary ones are. If you aren't sure, you can take some time to listen, and you'll soon find out. Knowing this, the way you respond to these concerns, frustrations, and objections should be tailored to your prospect or customer. These responses could include:

a) Logical responses
b) Funny responses

c) Story responses

d) Factual responses

If you are trying to answer objections from a logical person and you only have humorous responses prepared, you will not likely make the sale. Similarly, if you are dealing with a person who loves to tell stories, but you have logical responses, you again may not get the sale.

Try to come up with the appropriate responses in each of the four categories so that you are truly prepared. When you meet a logical person, use logic. When you meet a funny person, use humor. When you meet a storyteller, tell a story. When you meet a factual person, state the facts.

4. Closing scripts

Do you have what it takes to close the sale? Are you prepared? You can prepare your closes and test them until you find one that increases your closing ratio.

At this point, let's broaden the meaning of the word "scripts" to mean the "system" that you use to close the sale. You see, there are things you can say... and there are things you can do. Many times, it's the things that you do that prove that "actions speak louder than words". Here are some ideas to stimulate your thinking.

Research shows that car wash customers receiving a customer frequency 10 slot punch card are more likely to return for 8 additional washes to earn a free wash when their frequency card is given 2 "head start" punches for free. It turns out that giving customers (what they perceive to be) preferential treatment works psychologically in most business situations. See if this can be applied in various situations within your own business. Here are some more examples.

Waiters and waitresses can use candy to increase their tips. According to Monmouth University, waiters and waitresses can increase their tips by giving customers a piece of candy with their check (19.59% average tip vs. 18.95% with no candy). They can increase their tip even more by doubling up and giving two pieces of candy: 21.62% average tip.

But consider this: the study found that the tip could be increased even more by first giving a single piece of candy, then after turning to leave, turning back around and offering a second piece of candy. This artificial drama evidently makes diners feel like they've received special treatment—something ostensibly outside of the normal candy-giving protocol—which was rewarded with an average tip of 22.99%.

Think about that for a minute. First, if you're a waiter or waitress, head straight for Costco and load up on Andes mints. They only cost 6 cents each, and on a $50 check, the double mint-fake out is worth an extra $2.02 in tips. This one strategy could add $40 to $50 cash in the pocket of waiters and waitresses per shift.

How about these...

A magazine advertising sales rep could offer a second smaller ad to be run in the back of the publication the prospect is considering for free. *The key?* Wait until after the customer signs for the first ad, *then* give the free ad as an unexpected thank you gesture.

A lawn service company could unexpectedly knock on a customer's door and ask them if they'd like a flat of flowers that were "left over" from another job planted in their beds.

This isn't rocket science. The Law of Reciprocity is extremely powerful. Just find something that you can *give* to your customers for free that appears to be done as a special favor and watch their reaction. They'll become more loyal. They'll talk you up to their friends which will lead to referrals. And they'll just plain like you more.

5. Marketing scripts

In the advertising world, jargon has now started to dominate all marketing and advertising. Think of jargon as words or phrases that are drearily commonplace and predictable, that lack power to evoke interest through overuse or repetition, and that are nevertheless stated as if they were original or significant. In advertising, you see and hear jargon all the time.

Since businesses only have 30 seconds to try to convey what makes them special, they lump everything into jargon such as "largest selection," "most professional," "lowest prices," "highest quality," "best service," "fastest," "most convenient," "largest in the state," "more honest," "we're the experts," "we specialize," "works harder," "gets the job done right the first time," and "been in business for 40 years."

Now listen, I'm not saying that you shouldn't be those kinds of things. Those make up the foundation you want to use to build your inside reality. But consider this. If my marketing says that I offer high quality and great service, aren't those scripts drearily commonplace and predictable? Don't they lack power to evoke interest through overuse or repetition? Don't businesses state them as though it were original and significant? Does my inside reality (what really makes me good at what I do) really shine through? Can you tell specifically what makes me valuable to the marketplace when I say, "highest quality" or "best service"?

See, you simply can't describe, demonstrate, exhibit, reveal, or display your inside reality using jargon. It's impossible! And unfortunately, the result is an outside perception that you're no different than anyone else. There's absolutely no distinction, no separation, and no differentiation. None. You can't make your inside reality and outside perception match up when you use jargon like this.

In fact, let me give you a way you can easily and quickly evaluate your own marketing scripts to see if you're getting caught up in the jargon trap. This evaluation is what we call, " *Well, I would hope so.*"

When you make a claim, don't think about it in terms of the words coming out of your mouth. Think about it in terms of the words entering your prospect's ears. This will enable you to realize just how absurd most jargon sounds. Look at the messaging in your marketing, and then ask yourself if the prospect's immediate response might be, "*Well, I would hope so.*" Let me give you an example.

I saw a TV ad for a home remodeling company. Throughout the ad they continuously emphasized the fact that their work was of the highest quality, it was priced fairly, and they guaranteed 100% satisfaction. *Well, I would hope so.* Would you hire *any* remodeler who didn't provide all of those as a standard part of their service? Of course not. This is *all* jargon... drearily commonplace... lacks power to evoke interest through overuse or repetition.

How about this one from a consulting company: "Our training leads to change. We increase the productivity, performance, and profit of your company." *Well, I would hope so!* Does anyone hire a consultant for any other reason than to do those things? Most ads today are nothing more than a jargon-fest. Does this jargon tell you anything about this companies inside reality? What else would you expect them to say? Everyone is always going to say wonderful things about their company if they can get away with it.

The problem is that if your company has an exceptional inside reality and you're using the same jargon as everyone else, then the outside perception is that you're all the same. And that's when prospects default to the company offering the lowest price. Price now becomes the only determining factor.

When you use this simple evaluation, just ask yourself openly and honestly *why* anyone would choose you over your competition? Then evaluate your answer against the "well, I would hope so" evaluation. And finally, check out all your advertising and marketing materials, including your website. Do they pass the "well, I would hope so" evaluation, or are they *all* chock full of jargon? If they are, then you need to make changes.

I know of a kitchen remodeler that ran by far the most impressive remodeling company in his community. Every member of his crew had at least 15 years of remodeling experience, they were all certified sub-contractors, they had won multiple industry awards, they were the only kitchen remodeling company that provided not only a full satisfaction guarantee, but also a 10-year material and labor warranty on everything they did. They left the jobsite every night cleaner than when they first arrived. They also guaranteed they could remodel any kitchen in no more than 5 days—half the time of their competitors. This of course, meant far less disruption and inconvenience to the homeowner.

In short, their inside reality was literally second-to-none. But they had a huge marketing problem. Their marketing looked virtually identical to all their far less-worthy competitors. Their marketing said things like: "certified sub-contractors," "guaranteed satisfaction," and then a long laundry list of the work they performed, such as new cabinets installed, complete kitchen remodeling and so on. Oh, and get this, they accept Visa and Master Card! *Well, I would hope so!*

But then ask this question: Who else can say that? When the owner of this remodeling company was asked that very question, he got really defensive. He said, "There's no other remodeler that can begin to match the work we do! Our sub-contractors are far-and-away the best there is! No one, and I mean no one, can say what we say!"

Understandably, this contractor was extremely passionate and protective when it came to the superior company, he had worked so long and hard to develop over the years. So finally, to try to get the point across to him, he was asked to pull up the websites of his five biggest competitors and see what all of them were saying on their home page. Let's just say that his jaw hung open for about two minutes straight before he finally pointed at the screen and said, "Oh my gosh... look at this other company's website. I know this guy. He's terrible. But his site says the exact same thing as mine. In fact, I think he copied my site word-for-word!" He then looked at the other remodelers and saw that all their websites were virtually identical to his.

So, remember, it's not who can do what you do. It's "who can say what you say?" And if your marketing scripts are full of jargon, then sadly that answer is that all your competitors can.

6. Scripts for Point-Of-Sale Upsell, Cross-sell, and Downsell

Think of every selling possibility and adapt your scripts to meet those occasions. Do you want to upsell to a higher priced product or service? You should have your script ready to go. Has someone wandered into your place of business and is about to leave without buying anything? What downsell script could you use to at least begin the buying relationship?

Imagine this scenario: If 100 customers come into your store (or come to your website) every day and only 20 buy something, it means 80 of them don't buy. If you could convince just 1 out of those 80 to make a smaller purchase through your downsell strategy, then you'll have gained 21 customers instead of 20 and have possibly increased your revenue by 5%.

How might you articulate your offer?

"Excuse me, ma'am. Is this your first time in the store? Oh, it is? Then you qualify for our first-time shopper's discount." Do you think that might hook one or two of those 80?

7. Script locations – email, signs, websites, presentations, etc.

Have you applied your best and proven scripts to all your locations? How many locations do you have? How many marketing initiatives are you working and testing?

Think of the Parthenon in Greece. It has stood for over 2,400 years, partly because it has 46 outer columns or pillars and 23 inner columns—a total of 69. You want multiple "pillars" or initiatives because if one gets taken away, your business doesn't disappear.

8. Elevator Pitch

You might have just 30 seconds to sell someone—perhaps in an elevator before they reach the 7th floor. Are you ready with that speech so that by the time they reach their destination, they are ready to invite you into their office because they can't wait to hear more?

10 SECOND ELEVATOR PITCH TEMPLATE

(I / We) (action verb - *help, guide, teach, review, provide, consult with, present, aid, assist, support, grant, give, award, evaluate, assess*)

(negative emotions being experienced - *frustrated, furious, overwhelmed, clueless, demanding, frightened, desperate, struggling, angry, concerned, worried*)

(ideal client description - *dog lovers, young adults, chronic pain sufferers, overweight men, homeowners, business owners, brides-to-be, new mothers*)

who want to (what they want - *increase their profits, find an honest plumber, purchase that perfect diamond, find the relief they need, find the best deal*)

(solution - *discover a process, learn a fast and easy way, create the perfect solution, uncover the best method, determine the number* one reason, realize the best course of action, find the dramatic solution, locate the best deal, position themselves, place themselves first, find out everything they need to know)

to / so that they can (list 3 benefits - *live a pain free life, build the business of their dreams, finally give the perfect gift, feel they're getting the most value for the money they pay, pay the lowest price, receive the highest value, obtain the best guarantee, receive award-winning service, receive the highest level of expertise at the lowest possible price*).

30 SECOND ELEVATOR PITCH TEMPLATE

Do you know how... (list 2 to 3 negative emotions - *frustrated, furious, overwhelmed, clueless, demanding, frightened, desperate, struggling, angry, concerned, worried*)

(ideal client description - *dog lovers, young adults, chronic pain sufferers, overweight men, homeowners, business owners, brides-to-be, new mothers*) are

(what are their hot button is - *looking for a repair shop that is honest and fair, searching for a doctor who will spend more than 2 minutes with them, looking for long-lasting and possibly permanent pain relief, looking to buy that perfect "X"*)

but they (list 2 - 3 major frustrations - *have no clue if the price is fair, have no idea what they need, do not know who to trust, have no way to know if their being lied to or possibly ripped off*)?

134

What I do is... (action verb - *help, guide, teach, review, provide, consult with, present*) them with a

(overview of solution - *tested and proven method, quick and pain-free solution, revolutionary new procedure*) that

(solution to hot button - *immediately attracts more client, instantly relieves their pain, puts them in touch with the help they need*) so they can

(list 3 benefits to them - *live a pain free life, build the business of their dreams, finally give the perfect gift, find a contractor that won't rip them off*).

Example: Jeweler

What do you do?

10 Second Elevator Pitch:

"I provide clueless guys who want to purchase that perfect diamond learn a fast and easy way to instantly assess any diamond so that they can determine the ones with the highest quality, the lowest price and the boldest customer protection guarantee in the industry."

30 Second Version:

"Do you know how frustrated and clueless guys are looking to buy their loved one that perfect diamond, but they have no clue if the

price is fair or if the quality is high?

"What we do is teach them an instant assessment method that helps them buy the perfect diamond so they can get the highest quality, pay less than half the retail price, and receive the boldest guarantee in the industry."

Example: DUI Attorney

What do you do?

10 Second Elevator Pitch:

"I provide frightened and concerned first time DUI offenders who want to avoid a felony conviction and mandatory jail time with the means to receive probation instead of a criminal felony charge, only pay half the normal fine, and obtain the help they need so that they can rest assured this unfortunate event doesn't haunt them for the rest of their life."

30 Second Version:

"Do you know how the law punishes young adults who receive a DUI by threatening them with a felony conviction that stays on their record forever, as well as mandatory jail time combined with an outrageous fine that can run into the thousands of dollars?

What I do is represent first time offenders as a former prosecuting attorney who has excellent rapport with the current prosecutor and judge, and since it is mandatory that all my clients undergo *mandatory drug rehab therapy, I can guarantee that I can secure a plea agreement with no jail time, a maximum $1500 fine and 1 year of probation... at which time all charges will be dropped from the offenders record."*

9. Stadium Pitch

A "stadium pitch" relates to your opportunity to present to a large number of your choice prospects—this is a concept initially taught by the late Chet Holmes and it can be used in all your communications. If I were to put you in a stadium (or a Trade Show) with 5,000 of your best potential clients, would you be ready for that opportunity? Think about this: If you can prepare for that opportunity, you'll be ready for all the lesser ones as well, including the ones where you are speaking to one person at a time.

In truth, even when you speak to a group, you still need to speak to them as if you are speaking to them individually because people *hear* the message individually.

How do you approach this opportunity? Maybe this stadium full of people don't care about you or your solution. So how do you grip them from the start so that even those who don't care will sit up and listen because what you're delivering is of value?

One thing is for certain—you can't start talking about yourself or your company! You must start with a powerful story or question or a statement that stands against what they hold to be the norm. Then

137

you must lead them through an education so that they immediately see you to be the expert. And your education brings out the pain they're currently experiencing in a certain area of their life.

Only then do you show them what a perfect solution looks like.

And only after that do you show them why you are the ideal person to present that solution.

You see, the entire presentation script is strategic.

10. Answering Machine/Voice Mail

If you're calling a company and trying to get a hold of a decision maker, you should have scripts that you can easily read from that build trust and rapport and make the prospect want to call you back.

On your own voice mail, don't just say, "Leave a message." You have someone on the phone! Use the opportunity to educate and sell. Have you thought about this?

If you don't have any scripts at all, the best way to start is to have your best salesperson record their actual successful conversations with prospective clients. Then transcribe the words and put those words on the lips of the underperforming staff. Test them with a small portion of your staff and watch what happens. It the tests are positive, then make sure that the entire staff uses the same scripts.

Some companies develop great script books that their salespeople practice and use in all their selling encounters. Take the time and develop yours. There are no shortcuts here. The success of your sales and marketing depends upon it. Even small improvements in your scripts can lead to incremental (5% or more) improvements in your revenue.

Making it Practical

Take some time to think through these questions and then apply the most obvious solutions that would have an impact on your business.

If you had a script tree that your staff could use so that they would know what to say no matter which direction the conversation went, do you think that would help?

Next, what scripts could you add for the biggest immediate impact?

Then, what scripts could you implement in the next 12 months for the biggest long-term impact?

How to Find Easy Profits by Optimizing Your Close Rates

Close rates are a major point of leverage for improving revenue and profitability and have an immediate impact on sales. They can normally be improved by an in-depth examination of the sales process and the state (and implementation) of your policies and procedures.

If you know the processes and the corresponding metrics for your close rates, you can then take steps to improve upon your percentages. For example, you can look at:

- What your staff is saying
- How they build rapport
- How they handle objections

And then you can see the results.

However, if you're not tracking metrics, you're just letting your sales staff do whatever they want and then you're lucky to get anything at all.

Your staff will not *respect* your system if you don't set standards and *inspect* that which you've asked them to do. Combine that with the truism that it's nearly impossible to improve something if you don't measure it.

In our chapter on Policies and Procedures, I stated that it could be your company policy that each person in the business must write a "to do" list at the beginning of the month which they will break into weekly action plans, which will end up as daily "to do" lists. Then the manager will inspect what they have planned for the day and follow up at the end of the day to see what was accomplished. I had stated that this could raise productivity by 20%.

In this chapter, we'll look at your Initial Close Rate and then your Follow-up Close Rate. By looking at them separately, we'll get different insights into how we can best optimize them.

Initial Close Rate

Just as we stated that you could raise productivity by 20% by a simple daily inspection, your initial close rate can be refined as you look at the major components of closing the sale and create a series of "best practices" around the process. You might not know what the best practices are. However, the top salespeople should know what they are. These can be written down, tested, recorded, refined, and practiced or "drilled" until a level of excellence is reached across the sales team. Simply going through this process could improve the initial close rate by 10% or much more.

Components of the initial close that you review and refine include:
- The length and components of the sales cycle,
- The scripts that are employed (including overcoming

objections),

- The salesperson's belief in their product or service,
- Their level of enthusiasm,
- The value proposition that has been created,
- The risk-reversal that is used,
- The appropriate level of urgency that is created,
- The special promotion that can be offered.

What is your current initial close rate? It's important that you establish a baseline. If you don't have the exact number, begin with an estimate. Think of it this way: "If you got in front of 10 prospects, how many of those would you close on the first attempt?"

It's my guess that you might know what the problem is, and in most cases, people often know what should be done, but they just don't do it. Perhaps it's because they're lazy. Maybe they're too busy and important things "slip off the plate". Maybe they just forget, and the lack of training and policies doesn't reinforce the importance of the action.

Making it Practical

Simply answering these questions will allow you to see the possibilities for improvement.

How do you think it would improve your close ratio if you made it a policy and you could get reports on each salesperson to ensure that they had followed the policy?

What is your current system for closing the sale?

Is there one person in your business who is significantly better than others at closing the sale?

What has been your best practice to date?

Have you ever run a workshop to find ways to improve your ability to close the sale? (The key is that you don't have to have all the answers. However, your staff might have a lot of answers if you can only draw them out.)

Follow-up Close Rate

To get a greater understanding of the importance of follow-up, we must look back at some research mentioned previously.

- 48% of salespeople call once and give up.
- 25% call twice and quit.
- 12% make three calls and stop.
- 5% give up after the fourth call.
- Only 10% keep calling and they make 80% of the sales.

These numbers may be slightly different in your time and space. According to Scripted, 44% of sales people quit after the first follow-up attempt. It is still recognized that 80% of sales take at least five follow-up attempts.

Next, you must make your follow-up and bonding process a requirement and a procedure for each salesperson. Too often you will get into a prospect's office, and they will never hear from you again. Or you can wait too long after a meeting to follow up and they forget your name while you're waiting. In your weekly meetings, think about how you can better follow up with clients and with organizations to build better relationships.

To continue the bonding process, you need policies and procedures in this area. Leaving the follow-up process to the individual skills and moods of staff will prevent you from every being at the top of your market.

Imagine if you instituted some policies so that you knew how many times each of your people were to follow up, when they were connecting, and what they were saying?

Making it Practical

What is your follow-up procedure?

What is your follow-up close rate? For example, if you had 100 prospects and you closed 10 of them on the initial attempt (that's your initial close rate), how many of the other 90 would you close through follow-up attempts?

How many times do you follow up?

How many times *should* (or *could*) you follow up?

What would be the impact if you instituted some policies so that you knew how many times each of your people were to follow up, what they were saying, and you could get reports on each one?

Much of the implementation process in the recommendations in this chapter (and indeed throughout this book) require an ability to run a workshop with your employees. You, as the CEO, owner, or manager don't have to have all the answers. Often the correct solution can be drawn out from the employees who will then need to take some form of responsibility for implementation.

The process that you arrive at will be all-important for your consistency of action. Here is what you can easily do:

1) Tell your staff, "In three days we're going to discuss how to better <insert challenge>. I want each person to come with three ideas and the best idea will be rewarded with $50" (or whatever prize you think appropriate). This gives everyone time to think, discuss it with their spouse or friends and they'll come prepared with many more ideas than if you sprung the workshop on them at short notice.

2) At the meeting, you write all their ideas on the board without criticizing a single one. Criticism will shut down any positive energy you have in the group.

3) You vote on the best ideas, and you give it to one or two of the team to test!

4) IF the idea works, then you teach it to the group and you establish it as a policy.

5) Once you establish your written, formalized policies, you then police them, or "inspect" this activity until it becomes a habit.

Workshops can be run every week and are designed for the specific purpose of causing systematic and constant improvement in your business. Workshops could be the single most powerful way to harness every potential opportunity in your business.

When you run a workshop with your sales team and you ask them to come with better ideas how to improve their initial close rates and then their follow-up close rates, *they* will be the ones that bring you the best ideas.

To find a 5% or 10% impact here is practically child's play. It just takes a little focus and an ongoing commitment to optimizing your results.

Help Your Sales Team
Accelerate Their Results

A company must have sales to thrive. A sales team is a team of individuals, large or small, that work together to bring sales into the company. They are the bridge that brings the customer to the product. They are the ones that close the sale. Often a micro-business will not have a sales team, but there must be someone who functions in the role of sales. Perhaps it is the company owner.

An effective, finely tuned sales team can accelerate the growth of a company. Conversely, a team that underperforms in one or more areas limits the growth of the company and therefore the profitability.

In many industries, salespeople are seen as increasingly less valuable. People don't want to be sold to—they want to make their own decisions without any type of pressure. The role of "salesperson" is giving way to "client relationship manager" or other terms. One company owner knew that no one wanted to talk to a salesperson. It was tough for them to get in the door or get appointments. He gave each of his salespeople the title of "Assistant Director of Corporate Communications". A higher percentage of people were willing to talk to someone who was an Assistant Director of a company. And it gave the sales team an increased level of confidence.

There are many working pieces to the puzzle of the sales team, and we'll cover each one briefly. You can initiate each area your business if you don't have one, or you can refine what you do have.

1. Sales Model

Different companies have different sales models.

- Direct sales, which involves a person-to-person contact
  - o Inside sales where the salesperson remains in the company's location and makes phone calls or receives visitors.
  - o Outside sales where the salesperson goes out of the company location and meets people.
- Indirect sales, where there is no direct contact between a salesperson and a customer (vending machines, mail order, some online sales)
- B2B Sales where a business sells a product or service to another business
- B2C Sales where a business sells a product or service to an end user
- Channel sales, where salespeople sell through distribution channels

There are many iterations of this and many other sales models that could be included.

2. Sales Manager

Sales managers are responsible for the success and development of the team under them. They will hire (and fire) sales team members, facilitate their training, motivate them when necessary, set their goals and targets, develop (and oversee) policies and procedures, and administer rewards for successful work, or consequences for lack of success or inappropriate behavior.

3. Method of Compensation

A sales team could be compensated in any one of several different compensation models or formulas:

- Straight salary
- Straight commission
- Salary plus commission
- Rewards and bonuses

The method and formula will depend on several factors including business model, profit margins of goods sold, the industry or environment in which the business operates, the length of the sales cycle, and the level of risk involved in the process.

4. Superstars

Superstars are those rare salespeople that might outsell the next 5 or 10 salespeople combined. They have a driving desire to:

- Get immediate results
- Cause action
- Accept challenges

They also want:

- Power and authority
- Prestige and challenge
- Opportunities for individual accomplishments
- Opportunities for advancement
- Freedom from close controls and supervision

They can be difficult to find, difficult to manage, and difficult to keep. However, because they are so good at bringing in sales, they are given a measure of leeway because the company is afraid to lose them. They have strong egos but feed off encouragement. They dislike routine or mundane tasks which mean they might not fill out their reports or show up for sales meetings—they'll probably be out making sales. Find one or two and you'll make more money... while you pull your hair out in frustration.

5. Training

There are multiple steps to the sale, and you can offer training on each step.

1. Establish rapport,
2. Qualify the buyer,

3. Build value,

2. Create desire,

3. Overcome objections

4. Close the sale,

5. Follow up.

If you analyze the steps that a client or group goes through to decide to purchase, and then you break down those steps, and focus on improving them, you will become better and better at the process. For example, what can you do to establish better and faster rapport? How about building a higher perceived value in your product or service? What can you do to overcome objections in a much more thorough manner?

Sales managers will use their weekly meetings to drill down in at least one of these steps each week to help their team consistently improve.

6. Prospecting and Lists

Lists can be purchased from list brokers or built organically. To find a list to purchase, search Google for a reputable list broker. The best brokers will help you find and evaluate lists and refine your list strategy for direct marketing campaigns.

Often, the role of marketing is to build lists that can be given to the sales team to nurture and then close. There are many list-building "devices" available today, one of which is the lead-capture form on a landing page or website. The business gives you something of perceived value in exchange for your name and email address.

Many businesses collect names and contact information but do little with them. A business must have both the method to build a list and a system or procedure to engage with the list they have.

7. Dream Clients

Dream clients are those that have a major impact on your business. It could be that they spend much more than the average buyer, or they have extraordinary leverage or popularity. One dream client could be worth 10x or 100x the value of a "regular" client.

If you're selling books, you might want to get your book in the local bookstore, but a dream client would be Costco or Walmart.

If you're selling consulting services, you might consult for the local restaurant down the street, but a dream client would be Apple, Microsoft, IBM, McDonald's, or any Fortune 1000 company.

If you're selling homes, getting the listing for a celebrity (sports, movie, music, etc.) will elevate your business.

8. Trade Shows

Trade shows are simply the opportunity to connect with a multitude of potential customers in one place in a very short period. They require unique preparation, promotion, and strategy. www.TSNN.com gives you an extensive database of trade shows that you can attend.

You must determine why you want to go:

- Make sales
- Meet influencers in the industry
- Build lists
- Be seen as a thought leader by being a speaker

And you must determine how you are going to get the maximum ROI from the trade show. You must plan the steps you'll need to take:

- Before the event
- During the event
- After the event

9. Dealing with Decision Makers

It's the goal of every salesperson to get past the "gatekeeper" and speak directly to the decision maker. There are strategies to increase your ability to get to the decision maker and strategies to influence the gatekeeper more effectively—companies can find ways to increase their effectiveness in each area.

Powerful scripts are often the key to getting past the gatekeeper. Scripts can be refined and recorded, then role-played for increasing effectiveness.

Sometimes you know that you won't get to the decision maker on a visit so you must have a packet of material ready that the gatekeeper will pass along to the decision maker. What could you bring and leave with a gatekeeper that would cause him/her to say, "I think I should show this to my boss"? Perhaps it's a short 90-second video on a thumb drive. Maybe it's a corporate-style brochure with a headline that addresses the problem which that company is likely dealing with. Knowing your target audience is the key.

10. Closing the Sale

In my recent search with one of the shopping giants, there were 7,010 search results for "closing the sale".

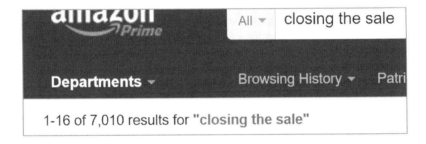

Advantage and opportunities to optimize profits can normally be found here by a simple investigative process—that is, analyzing the steps it takes to close the sale and finding ways to improve each step. If you pitch to 100 people and normally close just 20, your close rate is 20%. If you could find a way to close 21 out of 100, then you've grown your business by 5%. Taken together with the other improvements you might be able to make, this becomes an exponential impact on a business.

11. Order Fulfillment

Perfect order fulfillment is a company's ability to deliver their product or service to their customers within the timeframe that is expected (or sooner) with accurate documentation and no damages. This is not always easy to accomplish.

- A painter says he'll finish the project by the 30th of the month but takes an extra week.
- A supermarket runs out of a certain product on the shelf and must wait for new supplies to come in.
- A book is ordered but takes an extra day to arrive.
- A business consultant promises certain results, but they aren't realized.

A business needs good systems (and often partners with good systems) to be continually successful in this area. Systems must be monitored with religious diligence. Decisions makers must often act with speed to ensure that orders are fulfilled according to customer expectations. Leadership in management is the key to success.

12. Buyer's Remorse

Many times, following a purchase, the buyer will experience what is commonly known as "buyer's remorse"—they feel that they made a mistake in the purchasing decision, and they return the product or cancel the service.

Each company will have different strategies to reduce or limit buyer's remorse. A few examples are:

- A personal call a few hours after the purchase, thanking the customer for their wise decision,
- Building the perceived value during the sales process,
- Offering strong follow-up service.

Making it Practical

The idea of a running workshops was covered in another chapter of this book but it's useful to review again here because you can always find an impact with a sales team when you run a workshop.

You don't have to have all the answers. Often the correct solution can be drawn out from the employees who will then need to take some form of responsibility for implementation.

Here is what we do:

1) Tell your staff, "In three days we're going to discuss how to better establish rapport with a prospect. I want each person to come with three ideas and the best idea will be rewarded with $50" (or whatever prize you think appropriate). This gives everyone time to think, discuss it with their spouse or friends and they'll come prepared with many more ideas than if you sprung the workshop on them at short notice.

2) At the meeting, you write all their ideas on the board without

criticizing a single one. Criticism will shut down any positive energy you have in the group.

3) You vote on the best ideas, and you give it to your *best salesperson* to test! Why your best? Because if he or she can't succeed with it, then your average performers never will.

4) *If* the idea works, then your top performer teaches it to the group, and you establish it as a policy.

5) Once you establish your written, formalized policies, you then police them, or "inspect" the activities until they become habits.

Workshops can be run every week and are designed for the specific purpose of causing systematic and constant improvement in your business. Workshops could be the single most powerful way to harness every potential sales opportunity in your business and produce for you a finely tuned sales team.

What to Write on a Simple Postcard That Will Bring You an Avalanche of Customers

Here's a little-known marketing secret that involves using postcards to generate an avalanche of customers for your business. Let's say you're in the real estate business. Your postcards should say something like:

Dear Friend:

Would you like to learn an amazing secret that will allow you to buy property for 20% below what everyone else is paying?

If so, all you have to do is call 000-000-0000 and you will hear a free recorded message that reveals some truly amazing bargains.

Sincerely,

John Smith

Then write a telephone script. Practice it a few times... then record your script into your voice mail system. Once you're happy with it, you save it.

Your script will say something like this.

"Thank you for calling. My name is John Smith and I'd like to show you a few properties I have available that are being sold by people who are moving out of the area, and they must sell right away, no matter what. One property must be sold by next Wednesday and

another property I have must be sold by the following Tuesday, July 13th. I have some other fantastic properties in prime locations in the San Diego area that must be sold by certain dates as well because the owners are moving out of the region.

"If you'd like to learn more, just call me on my cell phone at 000-000-0000. I'd be happy to describe these properties to you and show them to you if this opportunity interests you."

Or there might be other reasons you have for why you're able to offer these properties at rock-bottom prices. But my point here is to show you the formula. You'll have your own story to tell, your own reasons, and your own deals to offer.

This message can be pretty long if you have a lot of interesting things to say. Some recorded messages run 10 minutes or more. Sometimes short and sweet is best. Sometimes longer is good if what you have to say is super interesting. Better short and sweet than long and boring. You want to create interest and intrigue, so they call you. Don't give them all the details.

Give them just enough so they'll want to call you and find out more. But give them enough detail so they believe you.

And that's a big part of effective copywriting and marketing. Tell an interesting story. And the story should be about why you're able to offer your prospect such a great deal. That's what makes you credible.

159

Once you've recorded your message, you then mail your postcards and wait for the phone to start ringing. And it will ring if you offer something along the lines of what I just described. Your prospects will always be interested in getting a bargain – something at a great price. The job of your script, and the story you tell on your recorded message, is to persuade your caller or your listener, that:

1. You really are offering a great price, a bargain they can't get elsewhere; and

2. You only have a few properties (or whatever you're selling) that fit this special situation criteria. Once the properties (or items) are gone, so is the special one-time opportunity.

Here's why this simple strategy works so well:

1. You're offering free insider information on what you know your prospect is interested in.

2. Your prospect is more likely to call when it's a recorded message than if they think they're about to be collared by a high-pressure salesman. The prospect knows they can just hang up on the recorded message, so they're much more likely to call.

3. When your prospect calls your recorded message hotline, they see that you're a good guy because you delivered what you promised – information on how to buy some great properties at rock-bottom prices. And your friendly, casual voice further reassures your caller and puts them at ease.

4. And you really have shown your prospect that you have a great opportunity for them – but one they'll miss if they fail to act now.

And, by the way, the tone of your recorded message is key. Just tell the story and state the facts. You should not sound like a street corner huckster. Just the opportunity you're offering in a very matter of fact, very calm, reassuring, and friendly manner.

I picked real estate in the previous example. But this formula works for any business.

If you're a plastic surgeon, here's some sample copy you might try for your postcard:

Dear Friend,

I'm using a new procedure that can make you look 15 years younger for a lot less than you think. Plastic surgery used to cost a small fortune.

But now almost anyone can afford it. It's very safe, and best of all, there's hardly any recovery time.

If you would like to learn more about this revolutionary new xxx procedure, just call 000-000-0000 and listen to the free recorded message for all the facts and details. You can call the recorded message anytime, 24/7.

Sincerely,

Dr. John Smith, MD

See the pattern? And notice that I used the old-fashioned courier typewriter font for my postcard. It's more personal looking, more friendly, looks more like a letter, and is more attention-getting. Tests show that courier still works better than Times Roman or the other desktop publishing fonts.

Here are a few more examples (just the first lines) to get you thinking in the right direction:

- "Would you like to learn how to play the piano in a week?"
- "It takes the schools two years to teach algebra. Would you like it if your child could learn the same material in just two months?"
- "I have a way to get you high-quality diamonds for less than a jeweler would pay for them?"

Think of your postcard as a teaser or a headline. If you have a knack for writing great, attention-getting, intriguing headlines, you can write great postcards that will generate lots of calls. It's all about emphasizing the big benefit to your reader. What's the big payoff for calling your recorded message hotline?

By the way, you can follow this same formula with your other advertising, not just postcards. You can run ads like this in the classifieds, in the Yellow Pages, and in little newspaper ads. And tiny ads like these are inexpensive to buy, unlike full-page display ads. You can also put text like this on fliers you distribute – even on your business cards, or on signs and billboards. And you can use this formula with your email marketing.

In addition to driving people to your recorded message hotlines, you can send them to your website.

But I love the recorded messages because they have your reassuring voice.

I'm sure you now get the formula. It's simple. Just apply it to your own situation. You can follow the exact same formula no matter what you're selling, and no matter what business you're in.

There is a great recorded message service that's designed for exactly this kind of program, and so much more. It's called **Automatic Response Technologies and it's** at:

https://automaticresponse.com/

This service not only makes it a whole lot easier than setting up a recorded message answering system yourself, but it will also give you a report on exactly who called. Even if the caller hangs up and never calls you, you'll know who did because you'll get a report with the names, phone numbers and the addresses of most people who call.

Now some people will block their numbers, so you'll miss those people. But most don't block their numbers, making this is a great way to build your list of highly qualified leads. You can then add these callers to your monthly newsletter list.

This program fits perfectly into an "Automatic Marketing" system. It's a very low-tech, simple way to automate a big part of your selling – to let machines do the lion's share of your selling for you, to let machines handle the initial sales presentations, to let machines do most of the sorting and sifting of your leads so that you yourself never again have to make another cold sales call.

You then just talk to those who are all set to buy from you. Try it. You'll get hooked on it.

A Strategy to Market Products or Services with Proven Results

In this chapter, you're about to embark on a journey. A journey into lateral thinking. I'll give you two examples and my challenge to you is not to write off these examples because they aren't from your exact same type of business. The power will come from seeing how you can extract these ideas and pull them into your own business to generate additional revenue.

The best way to sell products or services with a proven track record is through joint venture partnerships whose clients, customers or patients have a need for what you sell. However, for this strategy to work, you must know your product or service produces the results claimed by its manufacturer, and you should be able to predict specific (minimum) results over a fixed period (e.g., lose 10 pounds in 21 days, facial wrinkles disappear within 14 days, etc.).

If your joint ventures involve anyone in the medical community, position your product or service as a "clinical study." If it involves anyone outside of the medical field, position it as a "focus group".

Here's the basic premise. You want to sell your product or service and you need your joint venture partner (JV) to endorse you and represent you to their established database. On the other hand, your JV partner wants to generate additional leads for their business, and they can use your product or service with its proven results to do that.

165

Begin by creating a direct mail letter or email aimed at your targeted list of prospective JV partners and explain that you want to partner with them so you can both grow your businesses. Explain your product or service to them and how they can use it to attract new clients into their business through the offer of a free clinical study or focus group.

A total of 20 prospects (not current clients—have them use the study or focus group to generate fresh prospects) would be accepted into the program... 10 of them will use the product and 10 will be given a placebo. If possible, the first time this strategy is used with a new JV partner, the product or service as well as the placebo should be provided for free. There should be *no* initial cost to your new JV partner.

During the entire trial period, each participant should be assessed at specific intervals by the JV partner so they can build rapport and a relationship can be established. Done properly, the JV partner should be able to convert 30% (minimum) of the total participants into new paying clients for their business.

After the trial period, the 10 participants using the product will see the predicted results and will naturally want to continue using the product. The JV partner can then set up a landing page on their website where these new clients can order all future products and the JV receives an affiliate commission on each sale.

Next, publish the results the original 10 achieved to the 10 that were on the placebo. Once they see their results, they will want to use it as well. They will also be willing to purchase it, so they too can be directed to the website.

The End Result

Each JV partner can potentially add between 6 to 12 new clients to their business since they had more than ample time to establish a relationship as well as solid rapport with them during the trial period, and they also now have the potential for 20 new clients ordering your product or service on a regular basis which provides the JV partner with a lucrative passive income. They can now indefinitely duplicate these results by repeating this process over and over, continuously offering this same clinical study or focus group scenario and average the same number of new clients to their business and website transactions to grow their passive online income.

For you as the product or service provider, you now have up to 20 new customers buying your product or service through this affiliate partnership, and since the JV partner now has measurable and quantifiable financial results from the initial trial, you can now charge them each time they conduct their trial or study moving forward. You should also ask the JV partner for referrals as well.

Here's a specific example. Let's assume you're a chiropractor and you want to generate new clients. Unfortunately, you have no money for marketing. Here's what you do. Find a product or service that complements your practice such as health supplements, weight loss programs or perhaps colon cleanses. If you already offer these as the doctor, then that's great. If you don't, find one of these products that actually works and that has proven results. The proven results should include a specific time frame in which those results will be realized, such as lose 10 pounds in 21 days, or your facial wrinkles will disappear within 14 days and so on.

When you find the product or service that meets these criteria, contact the manufacturer or service provider, and explain this strategy to them. Tell them you will generate a minimum of 30 new customers for them each month in exchange for them providing you with 30 of their products at no cost to you (or at least at *their* cost).

Once you establish this relationship, create a list of complementary businesses that market to your target patient profile. So, for a chiropractor, complementary businesses might include massage therapists, rehabilitation clinics, retirement communities, acupuncturists, naturopaths or possibly health food stores.

Inform them you're offering a clinical trial in which every participant will receive a series of free products and services totaling $XXXX (this total is based on the retail price of the doctor's services and the retail price of the product or service you receive from the manufacturer you make the deal with).

These businesses should be willing to promote your clinical trial to their customers and database as a value add for their own business.

Their customers will see this as a valuable offer and credit the complementary business owner for recommending it to them. Why would anyone object to receiving an offer for $XXXX in free health services?

Here's how this clinical trial will be set up. A total of 20 prospects will be accepted into the program. 10 of them will receive the actual product produced by the manufacturer and 10 will receive a placebo. The chiropractor should *not* offer the clinical trial to current patients; they should use it to generate new patients. Remember, each participant in the trial is receiving everything for free. There should be *no* initial cost to them at all.

During the entire trial period, let's say in this case that's 21 days, each patient should be assessed at specific intervals by the chiropractor so the doctor can build rapport and establish a personal relationship. So, for the chiropractor, on day 1 of the trial they would have all 20 of the participants come into their office and the doctor would perform a full physical and a complete work up on each patient. They would *not* deliver a report of findings but just note on their chart any additional abnormalities the chiropractor knows can be corrected with future treatment.

The chiropractor's staff can do most of this, so the doctor doesn't have to invest their time except for the time required to build rapport and explain the program and its intended results to each patient. The doctor then meets with each patient again on days 5, 10, 15 and day 21. The trial is completed on day 21.

At each of these meetings, the doctor meets with each patient and takes relevant measurements that track the progress (or lack of progress for the placebo group) that each patient is attaining as they use the product or service provided by the manufacturer or service provider.

On day 21, the final assessment of results is completed, and the doctor meets with each patient for an in-depth "report of findings." Since the manufacturer's product produces proven results, the 10 participants using it will achieve those predicted results and will naturally want to continue using the product in the future.

And since they saw the exact results the doctor said they would experience, the doctor now has established massive pre-eminence in the eyes of that patient. The doctor can then present the additional physical problems they uncovered during their initial exam and enroll this patient into their main chiropractic treatment program, gaining a new patient in the process.

So, the chiropractor now has a new patient in their practice and has generated a new client for the manufacturer. Out of the 10 patients in the test group using the real product, 7 to 8 of the 10 patients should convert into new patients for the doctor and customers for the manufacturer.

The exact same process is repeated for all 10 members in the placebo group with one important exception. They're informed they were members of the placebo group, and their lack of results should be emphasized. They are then informed of the first group's results. Naturally, they will want to experience those results for themselves and will immediately want to order the product or service that was provided to the first group.

They will also receive special treatment offers from the chiropractor following their report of findings and thanks to the rapport and trust the doctor was able to establish over the consecutive meetings they held with them during the trial period, several of them will also convert into new patients in the doctor's regular treatment program.

The bottom line for the chiropractor is this: They gain 10 to 15 new patients for their practice and 10 to 15 (or more) new back-end product purchasers for the manufacturer. (Note that the chiropractor will know the exact numbers each trial will produce once they offer this clinical trial several times).

The chiropractor can then perform as many of these clinical trials as they so choose, often running three to five of them per month. Since each study lasts just 21 days, this strategy could produce 30 to 50 new patients for their practice every month along with the same number of new product purchasers for the manufacturer.

The typical chiropractic patient has a lifetime value of $2500, so just the patients alone are worth $75,000 or more *every month* to the chiropractor! If the back-end product or service nets the manufacturer a $50 monthly profit that would generate an additional $18,000 or more in annual passive revenue for every 3 sets of clinical trials the chiropractor conducts.

That's not too bad a rate of return for the chiropractor when you consider they're investing limited time and marketing dollars in this program. It's also a great rate of return for the manufacturer for investing in 10 free samples per trial.

The chiropractor has other options, however. They could become an affiliate with the manufacturer or service provider and pay them a wholesale price for their product or service and then sell it themselves at the retail price and create a lucrative passive income on the back end.

The doctor could then reduce their involvement by setting up a landing page on their website where their new clients can order all future products and the chiropractor receives an affiliate commission on each sale. The doctor could then send out an email or direct mail letter to their entire patient database informing them of the superb results the clinical trials are producing and further compel additional patients to buy their supplements.

The chiropractor could also set up a continuity program where they offer to provide the manufacturers product or service monthly. They could offer a discount for a one-year commitment and set up the payment collection and product or service delivery on a pre-set schedule that would be hands-free to the doctor. This also provides a lucrative passive income to the doctor.

If the doctor averaged just 20 patients on this program every month, after 12 months they would have 240 patients in this continuity program. If the doctor was making a profit of only $20 per patient per month, they would be making $4,800 per *month* ($57,600 per year) at this point, and that number would continue to grow into the future. Note: this is passive income only and does *not* consider the additional patients produced for the practice.

Once the chiropractor performs a series of these clinical trials and collects documented results, they will begin to generate specific results that fall within specific parameters. For example, they will discover that for every clinical trial they hold, they will generate "on average" 15 new patients for their practice and 18 new customers for their supplements.

They can also assign a revenue figure to those numbers and then project that number over 5 years (the average life of a small business).

Now for the million-dollar question... do you suppose other chiropractors might be interested in doing this exact same thing? Do you think those other chiropractors would be willing to pay a setup fee of perhaps $10,000 and a monthly licensing fee of $397 for the rights to continue to license this process from the original chiropractor?

If you were a chiropractor, would you pay $10,000 and then $397 per month for someone to hand you a proven and tested way to add $250,000 in additional revenue *per year* to your practice?

The chiropractor can now duplicate these results indefinitely by repeating this process over and over, continuously offering this same clinical trial, and averaging the same number of new patients to their business and website transactions to grow their passive online income.

It's important to emphasize that any chiropractor can use this strategy whether they partner with the manufacturer so there's no out-of-pocket cost to them at all, or if they decide to buy from the manufacturer at a wholesale price as an affiliate.

They should look at the vast universe of health supplements and health related products or services and select the one they feel most comfortable with, and then verify it will produce the stated results. These could entail health supplements that improve energy or eliminate joint pain, they may be for weight loss, or possibly to stop smoking.

The doctor could then contact the health supplement company and form a JV or affiliate relationship with them. Since the supplement company is going to be receiving a bevy of new clients for *no* advertising costs, they should agree to provide the doctor with free product for the 10 clinical trial patients that will receive that product versus the placebo group.

The chiropractor could generate prospective patients through JV relationships in their local community as I previously explained.

But this exact same strategy can be applied to most any business if you put some thought and innovation into applying it. The basic concept is you're offering a product or service for free that produces a guaranteed and specific result that appeals to your target prospects and that you feel can produce the promised results at least 90% of the time. Then you only need to invest your time to establish trust, respect, and rapport with each prospect as stated in this strategy.

As an additional example, let's say you own a carpet store. Your main means of advertising is to run expensive TV and radio commercials and the high cost of marketing is eating up all your profit. Let's think creatively how we could adapt this exact same strategy to this carpet store.

First, ask yourself as the carpet store owner who it is that would have direct access to prospective carpet buyers. The answer for me would be carpet cleaning companies. They're in hundreds of people's homes every single day and can determine who needs new carpet and who doesn't. Here's what needs to happen next.

The carpet store needs to create an offer to homeowners that would generate additional sales for the carpet cleaning company that in turn will produce a higher demand for new carpets. This means the carpet would need to be in such filthy condition that it either requires

175

cleaning (benefits the carpet cleaning company) or it needs replacement (benefits the carpet store).

By helping the carpet cleaner generate more prospects the carpet store will generate more business for themselves if the carpet cleaner agrees to endorse them and actively sell their carpet services. By offering the carpet cleaner a way to generate more leads, they will be more than willing to actively endorse the carpet store.

So how can the carpet store help the carpet cleaner show a homeowner they have additional carpet in their homes that needs cleaning? By doing some basic research, the carpet store discovers that when you shine a black neon light on carpet, it reveals every spot where a pet has urinated on that carpet. For most homeowners with pets, this is a very common condition that most of them have no idea has taken place.

Naturally, when their carpet lights up like a neon sign, they can't request cleaning services fast enough. And in many cases, the carpet is so filthy they just want it out of their homes and to have it replaced. That's when the carpet cleaners can hand the homeowner a special VIP voucher good for either a discount or special value-added services that makes the carpet store a no-brainer choice for them to buy their carpet.

The carpet store can develop everything the carpet cleaners need, including providing them with the neon lights and a compelling script to use when selling their services. This establishes massive reciprocity with the carpet cleaners who are then actively endorsing the carpet store to every homeowner they meet.

By following this script, the carpet cleaners can offer this special pet detection service to the homeowner's neighbors *while* they're at their home cleaning the carpet. This could produce an additional 3 to 5 homes they could inspect before they leave the original job. Out of those 5 homes, there's an excellent chance they will pick up 2 to 3 additional jobs, with *no* marketing dollars involved.

Think any carpet cleaner would more than welcome an opportunity to double or triple their revenue for *zero* marketing expense?

And one more thing to consider. Once this carpet store implements this marketing process for their own store and documents the results they produce with it, do you think other carpet stores would be willing to pay for the rights to learn about and license a proven and tested turnkey system for generating a multitude of new prospects and customers?

The original carpet store could then license their process to other carpet stores and charge a substantial setup fee and monthly rights to use their proven and tested marketing program.

This strategy can be adapted to work for any business in any industry. It simply requires a little thought, planning, research, and innovation... just like the carpet store did.

Steal My Bold Promise in Limited Time Strategy

Lead generation involves the finding of prospects and convincing them to provide you with their name and other data. Done properly, it identifies your highest quality leads and locates where they can be found. When you know the proper strategies and tactics required to get them to respond, your revenues, sales and profits will soar.

First, you *must* know and understand what marketing is really supposed to do:

- Grab the reader's attention,
- Facilitate their information gathering & decision-making process,
- Provide a specific, low risk, easy to take action that helps them make a good decision.

All marketing must grab the prospect's attention. If it doesn't, it's worthless. They'll never read, watch, or listen to the rest of the ad. That means you must have a great headline if the ad is in print. If it's on the radio, it's the first thing they hear; if it's on TV, it's the first thing they see and hear. When you're communicating with your prospects, the "headline" is your bold claim.

Second, all prospects, no matter who they are or what they're buying, are always looking for the best deal. That doesn't mean lowest price; it means the most value for the price. They will pay a higher price for increased value. To know if something is the best deal, they must have decision-making information.

Your marketing *must* help the customer gather information that aids them in their decision-making process. That's why the target customer profile and their thought process are so important. Without these fundamentals in place, you won't know the right information to provide them.

And third, your marketing must contain a low, or no risk offer to further facilitate their decision-making process. You must give them a compelling, yet safe way to take the next step. That next step may be to buy what you sell if you sell a lower priced product or service. If you sell expensive items, that next step may be to simply request additional information.

These three principles must always be present if your marketing is going to be effective.

One of the best ways to generate leads is to make a bold promise of results that can be achieved in a very limited time frame. This instantly captures the attention of your target prospects. A bold promise compels them to want to know more about what you sell.

Perhaps offer them an assessment of their current situation or problem, along with the claim you can provide a solution to that situation or problem within a limited time frame. This could also be accomplished using a webinar or a free report. Here's the basic process you want to follow:

Step 1: Communicate to them your "bold claim"

- Identify a way that will allow you to demonstrate your value,
- Show you can help the prospect in X minutes (or at least convince them you can),
- If done correctly, you can convince them to give you additional time,
- At the very least, use this limited time demonstration to obtain a second appointment.

The basic premise of your demonstration is to convince them in XX minutes that there are four things they can do immediately that will produce Y results.

Step 2: Create a compelling script

It should build interest in your offer by promising them there's a solution to their problem or situation. (The bold claim in step 1 focuses on their problem; step 2 promises them a solution).

Consider this potential voice mail script:

"If you're considering jumping back into the stock market because you're fed up with the low interest being paid on CD and other financial instruments, then there are 3 things you MUST know to keep you from losing your shirt. When it comes to high return investing, Guaranteed Return Stock Trading is the best

method you can use. It's making fortunes for those who are currently using it. It's simple to learn and easy to apply, and I can show you the exact process in just 18 minutes. During that short time frame, I'll teach you three trading secrets used by the pros that you can use to immediately increase your net worth by at least 25%."

- Notice above that your promise *must* be specific,

- You *must* deliver on your promise within the allotted time frame,

- You *must* stop at the time you said you would or risk losing your credibility.

Step 3: Come up with 3 or 4 questions

These can provide you with the information you need to provide your prospects with the value you're promising (create a short form assessment questionnaire).

Show them how you *can* deliver X results or how you *could* have delivered X results based on historical data.

Step 4: Overcome any objections

Most prospects are initially skeptical of bold claims, and rightfully so. The limited timeframe you're promising is designed to convince them to "give you the chance to prove yourself.

Develop a script that says something like this...

"Listen, I know this may sound too good to be true, especially since everyone today is telling you they can help you achieve remarkable results, and then of course, none of them ever do. I want to assure you the results I will help you achieve in that short time frame are real and substantial, and I can produce these results in just 18 short minutes. Here's how I'm going to do that. We've developed 3 fundamental trading strategies that every investor should be using for every trade they make... but not one of them do.

"As we've worked with hundreds of stock and day traders, our experience has been that less than 5% know anything about these strategies. By simply implementing them on your next trade, they increase the average trade value by at least X%. I can get you these exact same results in just 18 minutes, and I only need to ask you 3 simple questions."

Step 5: You *must* stop at time frame you set.

If you promise to deliver specific results in 18 minutes, you *must* be able to do exactly that. You can bet your prospect will be timing you to see if you keep your word to them. After all, they have granted you this time because of that limited time promise you made to them. You might say something like this:

"Well, I've just noticed we're at the 18-minute mark. When we started, I promised you I wouldn't take up any more of your time. Unfortunately, I was just getting to an additional strategy that I felt would add an

182

additional XX% of profit to your daily trades. May I continue for an additional minute or two?"

Or

"OK... we're at the end of the 18 minutes I promised you. If you recall, my objective was to deliver 3 strategies we use to help stock traders make more money... and that those 3 strategies would help you increase your daily results by XX amount. Do you now see how you can easily attain these amazing results?

If yes...

"Great, so now you have two choices. I can continue while your situation is fresh in my mind, and I can show you the entire program so you have all the information you need to make an informed decision... or we can schedule a second meeting and go over everything then. If I continue now, I only need an additional [X] minutes, but I want to make sure I have your permission first."

If they say they don't have time, set up a specific follow-up meeting or whatever specific action would be appropriate as the next step (send them a report, attend a webinar, etc.).

If they agree to a follow-up meeting, be sure you send them an email and outline your discussion with them, highlighting the results you uncovered for them and reinforce the major benefits they will receive from what you're selling.

Say something like:

"Hi (fname), it was certainly my pleasure speaking with you today. I'm looking forward to our meeting next Monday where I can show you how to achieve even greater results than what we uncovered in our 18-minute meeting.

"During that meeting, we discovered that you weren't following the 3 strategies I outlined and explained to you, and as a result, you were losing, on average, $XXX dollars per day that you could have been putting into your pocket instead. We also managed to determine that if you immediately implemented our 3-step program, you would see an instant revenue increase of XX% every month through your trading account. And we did all of that in only 18 minutes. Do you realize that we're just getting started? Wait until you see the results, I can help you get after our next meeting."

It's also a great idea to send them an additional email the day of the actual meeting to again reinforce the benefits and keep their interest level high.

Remember, your job is to provide every prospect you meet with or speak to with massive value using a demonstration. I know of a chiropractor once who said,

"I help massive pain sufferers who have been told by their doctor that they suffer from Fibromyalgia... the most misdiagnosed illness on the planet... to discover if

they really do have this dreaded disease by offering them a revolutionary new diagnostic procedure that has a 97.3% accuracy rate in properly diagnosing this horrible condition. Give me 7 minutes of your time and I'll set your mind at ease and help you get rid of the real pain for good."

You can also use a similar script as a phone survey. Call prospects to ask them about the things they want or need that can improve their situation, solve a problem or better their life, like the Fibromyalgia sufferers

"We're looking for 10 Fibromyalgia sufferers to participate in a free clinical study that can finally confirm their diagnosis as well as dramatically relieve their pain. May I have your permission to continue?

Have three or four specific questions scripted out that will grab their attention and get them interested in participating with you.

I just gave you two examples in this chapter. A mistake would be to dismiss it as not applicable to you. A better idea would be to meet with your business coach or a teammate and dialogue about how you might extrapolate the ideas in this chapter into your individual business situation. There's tremendous power by "seeing" things that your competitors have never thought about.

Made in the USA
Middletown, DE
28 August 2022

72507867R00106